T0306057

Corporate Governance in India

This book looks at how we can promote better governance practices in business organizations in developing economies. It presents a mix of conceptual perspectives and observations on corporate governance practices in a concise manner and illustrates through empirical evidence drawn from the Indian business environment. The secondary data analysis provides insights into Indian firms' corporate governance practices. This book is a useful reference for anyone who wishes to identify leading practices and develop broad recommendations applicable to corporate governance practices in developing economies in general.

Arindam Das is Associate Professor at the IFMR Graduate School of Business, Krea University, Chennai, India. He has more than 25 years of professional experience, including consulting assignments, senior managerial roles, executive training and academic responsibilities in business schools. His current focus areas in research and teaching include corporate governance, M&A/EJV performance, international business and technology-led business transformation. He holds a PhD from the Indian Institute of Foreign Trade, New Delhi, and he is a certified independent director with the Institute of Directors.

Routledge Studies in Corporate Governance

For more information about this series, please visit www.routledge.com/Rou-
tledge-Studies-in-Corporate-Governance/book-series/RSCG

Corporate Governance in India

Arindam Das

Routledge
Taylor & Francis Group

LONDON AND NEW YORK

First published 2020
by Routledge
2 Park Square, Milton Park, Abingdon, Oxon OX14 4RN

and by Routledge
52 Vanderbilt Avenue, New York, NY 10017

Routledge is an imprint of the Taylor & Francis Group, an informa business

First issued in paperback 2021

British Library Cataloguing in Publication Data
A catalogue record for this book is available from the British Library

Library of Congress Cataloging-in-Publication Data
A catalog record for this book has been requested

ISBN: 978-1-138-58112-8 (hbk)
ISBN: 978-1-03-209053-5 (pbk)
ISBN: 978-0-429-50689-5 (ebk)

Typeset in Times New Roman
by Taylor & Francis Books

Dedicated to the memory of my parents who encouraged me to learn through reflection, and to my wife and daughter who are my source of inspiration.

Contents

Figures

Tables

Abbreviations

CA2013	Companies Act 2013
CAPM	Capital Asset Pricing Model
CE	Circular Economy
CEO	Chief Executive Officer
CFO	Chief Financial Officer
CII	Confederation of Indian Industries
CMIE	Centre for Monitoring Indian Economy
CSR	Corporate Social Responsibility
EHS	Environment, Health and Safety
FDI	Foreign Direct Investment
FY	Financial Year
GRI	Global Reporting Initiative
HSD	Honest Significant Difference (Tukey's Test)
ICSI	Institute of Company Secretaries of India
IPO	Initial Public Offering
LODR	Listing Obligations and Disclosure Requirements of SEBI
MANOVA	Multiple Analysis of Variance
MCA	Ministry of Corporate Affairs, Govt. of India
MD	Managing Director
MoU	Memorandum of Understanding
NCLT	National Company Law Tribunal
NSE	National Stock Exchange
OECD	Organisation for Economic Cooperation and Development
PBDITA	Profit Before Depreciation, Interest, Tax and Amortisation
PCAOB	Public Company Accounting Oversight Board, USA
POE	Privately Owned Enterprise
ReSOLVE	Regenerate, Share, Optimize, Loop, Virtualize and Exchange Framework of Circular Economy
RPT	Related Party Transactions
SCORES	SEBI Complaints Redress System
SEBI	Securities and Exchange Board of India

SEC	Securities and Exchange Commission, USA
SOE	State Owned Enterprise
SOX	Sarbanes–Oxley Act
TBL	Triple Bottom Line

Part I
Introduction

1 Business model, strategy, governance and performance of the firm

Purpose of the firm and its business model

Way back in 1937 Ronald Coase asked a fundamental question about the purpose and existence of firms in his paper, "The nature of the firm." The essential idea behind his question was why certain economic activities take place within a firm and not as transactions in the market (Fontrodona and Sison, 2006). Of course, Coase came up with an explanation – a firm essentially is an instrument in the service of economic efficiency.

Taking Coase's argument further, one would ask, how and why the firm reduces the cost of production and what makes it more cost-effective than market transactions, and can we take it for granted that the firm, by its very existence, minimizes transaction costs?

Further theory developments, especially the concept of the principal-agent relationship within the firm, resource based views, and the fact that a firm is essentially a complex web of players and interactions, explain how firms are able to reduce costs in certain situations, and how in certain instances they would not be able to achieve economic efficiency. This may also explain, albeit partially, why costs and value created are different for any given set of firms, even though they operate in similar environments with similar resources.

Thus, one of the primary challenges for management and business professionals is about creating superior value for the firm in a competitive marketplace and sustaining this superior value creation. The concept of the business model is useful in explaining how superior value could be created by a firm. The key functions of a business model are to articulate the firm's value proposition by reflecting on management's hypothesis in defining the ways the enterprise delivers and captures value: identify a market segment, and define the structure of the value network required by the firm to create and distribute the offering (Teece, 2010). A sustainable business model involves segmenting the market, specifying the revenue generation mechanisms for the firm, estimating the cost structure and profit potential of producing the offering, describing the position of the firm within the value network, linking suppliers and customers, identifying potential complementors and competitors, and finally it should formulate the competitive strategy by which the firm will gain and hold advantage over its rivals.

Firm performance and role of strategy

When we study business organizations, we observe significant variation in their performance. It varies for firms with similar resources and capabilities within the same industry sectors, having been subjected to similar external stimuli and constraints, and it varies with time as well. And, over time, some business organizations get wiped from the market, while others continue to create value, and they evolve as the business environment and opportunities change. For example, Japan's Sumitomo group, which is a conglomerate today, traces its origins back to the copper mining business in the early 17th century. In essence, the most efficient and effective companies win.

Researchers argue that the strategies a company pursues have a major impact on its performance relative to its competitors. In addition, to create sustained superior value for its owners as well as other stakeholders, a firm must engage in business model innovation, coupled with strong strategy formulation and execution practices. A firm's managers, under the guidance of the leadership team, carry out analysis of pertinent information to identify appropriate strategies for the firm, and implement them to achieve sustained competitive advantage.

A strategy formulation process primarily involves reviewing the firm's existing business model, its mission, vision and goals, and subsequently carrying out analyses of the external business environment and internal environment. The external business environment analysis helps the managers identify threats and opportunities, and the internal business environment analysis helps the firm recognize its strengths and weaknesses, associated with its people, processes, capabilities and resources, both financial and non-financial. Such environment analysis helps the firm to make the right strategic choices. Next, the firm develops its corporate-level strategies which define the broad contours of its business activities and inter-relationship among business divisions, business-level strategies which deal with developing competitive advantage in the products and services it offers to the customers, and function-level strategies which help improve the functional capability of people and the organization.

In contrast to the strategy formulation process, which is primarily analytical and involves decision-making at the highest level, the strategy implementation process is essentially operational in nature, and involves almost the entire workforce who execute the strategic decisions taken at the formulation stage. It also involves designing organization structure, developing an organizational culture, and the processes and control systems to measure and evaluate performance.

The three jobs of management, according to Peter Drucker, are managing a business, managing managers, and managing workers and work (Drucker, 2012). Thus, successful companies transform key management processes to focus not only on strategy formulation and implementation, but also on organizational alignment and workforce alignment, strategy communication, and promoting best practices. In doing so, the company positions itself uniquely in the competitive landscape, and creates value in a sustainable manner.

Importance of governance

Having deliberated on the role of business models and strategy in capturing and delivering value for the organization, we need to explore the importance of governance in value creation.

The Cadbury Committee, UK defines governance as:

> a system of rules, procedures and processes by which a company is directed and controlled. Specifically it is a framework by which various stakeholder interests are balanced and efficiently and professionally managed. (Cadbury, 1992)

In other words, governance is the process of determination of the broad uses to which organizational resources will be deployed and the resolution of conflicts among the multitude of participants in organizations (Daily, Dalton and Cannella, 2003). The context is critical due to the diversity of participants in a modern organization. A modern organization is run by a management team that is responsible for carrying out the management functions. However, while this management team runs the day-to-day operations and takes decisions on behalf of the company, it normally does not include the owners of the company. The owners and the management team are typically bound by a principal-agent contract whereby the management team is the agent of the principal, i.e., the owners, and it is the agent's responsibility to act and make decisions that creates and captures maximum value for the owners.

The Organisation for Economic Cooperation and Development (OECD) defines corporate governance as:

> Corporate Governance involves a set of relationships between a company's management, its board, its shareholders and other stakeholders. Corporate Governance also provides the structure through which the objectives of the company are set, and the means of attaining those objectives and monitoring performance are determined. (OECD, 2015)

The OECD acknowledges the multi-dimensionality of the relationship that exists between the interested parties in the organization. It is not merely a

principal-agent relationship. A comprehensive definition of corporate governance is provided by the Institute of Company Secretaries of India (ICSI) as:

> Corporate governance is not just corporate management; it is something
> much broader to include a fair, efficient and transparent administration
> to meet certain well-defined objectives. It is a system of structuring,
> operating and controlling a company with a view to achieve long term
> strategic goals to satisfy shareholders, creditors, employees, customers
> and suppliers and complying with the legal and regulatory require-
> ments, apart from meeting environmental and local community needs.
> When it is practised under a well laid out system, it leads to the building
> of a legal, commercial and institutional framework and demarcates the
> boundaries within which these functions are performed. (Arya, Tandon
> and Vashisht, 2003)

As a multitude of players with differing objectives, some with executive
powers and others without, tend to drive decisions and actions at the firm, it
becomes necessary to align on the broad objectives of the firm, how they need
to be achieved and measured. The modern business enterprise distinguishes
between the providers of capital to the firm and the managers, who make and
execute decisions. Thus, corporate governance deals with protecting the
interests of the owners and others who bring in capital, monitoring the
activities of the executive management, and setting broad directions to the
executive management. It also becomes important to comply with applicable
regulatory frameworks, and address the needs of the larger external stakeholders, who could be impacted by the business activities of the firm – the
firm must realize that it is part of society and owes certain responsibilities to
that society. The presence of strong governance standards provides better
access to capital, which aids economic growth for the firm.

To summarize, the business model deals with the building blocks of a firm's
business, and strategic functions deal with the firm's unique positioning, trajectory and supervision of implementation of strategic initiatives. In contrast,
as Capasso and Dagnino (2014) suggest, the governance function deals with
the congruence assessment between the firm's chosen strategy and the interests of the owners and other relevant stakeholders represented in the board of
directors, and the effective appraisal of managerial actions.

In the following chapters we explore the theoretical underpinnings of corporate governance, and evolution of practices, regulations, and frameworks.

References and further reading

Arya, P. P., Tandon, B. B., & Vashisht, A. K. (2003). *Corporate Governance*. New
Delhi: Deep and Deep Publications Pvt. Ltd.
Cadbury, A. (1992). *Report of the Committee on the Financial Aspects of Corporate
Governance (Vol. 1)*. London: Gee & Co. Ltd.

Capasso, A., & Dagnino, G. B. (2014). Beyond the "silo view" of strategic management and corporate governance: Evidence from Fiat, Telecom Italia and Unicredit. *Journal of Management & Governance*, 18(4), 929–957.

Daily, C. M., Dalton, D. R., & Cannella Jr, A. A. (2003). Corporate governance: Decades of dialogue and data. *Academy of Management Review*, 28(3), 371–382.

Drucker, P. (2012). *The Practice of Management*. London: Routledge.

Fontrodona, J., & Sison, A. J. G. (2006). The nature of the firm, agency theory and shareholder theory: A critique from philosophical anthropology. *Journal of Business Ethics*, 66(1), 33–42.

Leblanc, R. (2016). *The Handbook of Board Governance: A Comprehensive Guide for Public, Private, and Not-for-Profit Board Members*. Hoboken, NJ: John Wiley.

OECD (2015). *G20/OECD Principles of Corporate Governance*. Paris: OECD Publishing. https://doi.org/10.1787/9789264236882-en. Last accessed 7 April 2019.

Teece, D. J. (2010). Business models, business strategy and innovation. *Long Range Planning*, 43(2–3), 172–194.

2 Theories and models of corporate governance

Essential elements of governance

In Chapter 1 we studied how corporate governance integrates with the functions of management and strategic planning to create and capture value.

The four key elements of corporate governance are transparency, responsibility, accountability, and fairness. Transparency deals with ensuring timely, adequate, and accurate disclosure of all material information. These disclosures must be over and above the statutory provisions given under rules and regulations. In fact, corporate governance's fundamental objective is not only the fulfilment of the legal requirements, but also ensuring the board's commitment to managing the company in a transparent manner for creating value.

Apart from ensuring transparency, the board has to take responsibility for its decisions: it has to balance its overall responsibility to shareholders with obligations to other stakeholders affected by the board's decisions and actions. In addition, the board of directors are accountable to the shareholders and extended stakeholders for the activities of the company. Lastly, fairness deals with fair and equitable treatment of all shareholders, including minority shareholders. In the next section we will explore how different theories of corporate governance uphold these elements.

Key theories of governance

Adam Smith, the legendary economist of the 18th century, once said:

> The directors of companies, being managers of other people's money, cannot be expected to watch over it with the same vigilance with which they watch over their own. (Tricker and Tricker, 2015)

The statement summarizes the underlying tension among the stakeholders in an organization, specifically, the tension between the owners and the executives. Over the past century several management theories have been developed that explain how corporate governance works and should work. In this section we will briefly review key theories that have shaped organizations' actions and policies in relation to corporate governance.

Agency theory

The quote from Adam Smith above underscores one of the fundamental challenges of governing an organization. As the owners of the organization ("principals") engage a group of non-owners ("agents") to run the organization, the agency problem creeps in. The executives, chosen as agents, may not pursue the objectives and intents of the principals; they may pursue their own agenda that enhances their own managerial empire and stature. In other words, the principals (owners) incur "agency costs" when they execute contracts with agents (directors). Agency cost can be defined as the extent to which returns to the owners fall below what they would be, if the owners themselves exercised direct control of the corporation.

There is empirical evidence that the agency problem does exist in many organizations, especially with listed public limited companies, where shareholders have no specific role in running the organization, and the board of directors takes practically all important decisions. Directors are found to treat the companies as their own properties, exploit their decision-making powers and receive undue benefits and remuneration from the company (Monks, 2008). In addition, as the risk of losing any personal wealth is nil, directors often indulge in extreme risk-taking and speculative decision-making.

Information asymmetry is another factor that contributes to the agency problem. Since directors, especially executive directors, are involved in the day-to-day operations of the company, while owners stay away from these activities, the owners have limited insight into the challenges and opportunities facing the organization. As a result, the owners are dependent on the directors for information and the directors may choose to share information selectively.

Though agency problems cannot be wished away, organizations can adopt certain broad mechanisms to minimize agency costs (Fernando, 2012). One of these is insistence on fair and accurate financial disclosures, which ensure that the owners or shareholders have access to all necessary information about the company's performance and operations, certified by independent, statutory auditors. Another includes greater emphasis on the effectiveness of independent directors on the board. Independent directors may not have any pecuniary motive regarding decisions that put shareholders' interests at stake.

While we have sufficient evidence to support agency theory, there are criticisms as well. Agency theory makes assumptions about the inherent characteristics and morality of all human beings, i.e., that people are more interested in personal goals than larger interests.

Stewardship theory

Stewardship theory posits a diametrically opposite view to that of agency theory, discounting any possible conflict between the executives and the owners of the organization. The theory argues that the owners nominate and appoint the directors, who then act as stewards for their interests. In other words, the basis of engagement is trust, and the directors have a fiduciary responsibility to act as stewards of the owners' or shareholders' interests.

Directors, as stewards, are expected to behave in a collectivistic, pro-organizational and trustworthy manner. Their motivations revolve around higher-order, intrinsic needs, pursuing performance improvement of the organization with a long-term association with the organization. This is in sharp contrast to the arguments of agency theory, where we perceive executives to be opportunistic and self-serving, with limited attachment to the long-term interests of the organization.

Though stewardship theory has been supported by numerous organizational studies, there are questions about its applicability in the current context of public limited companies. In the 19th century, a joint-stock, limited liability firm had a limited set of shareholders and they would choose their stewards to run the firm – trust, alignment and convergence of interests between the owners and executives was possible. In the current business environment, the shareholders of any large public limited company consist of various types of entities: from promoters, to pension funds and small retail shareholders. Considering that the owners themselves constitute a heterogeneous group with diverse purposes, and the fact that most of the owners have a limited role in identifying potential directors, it is impossible to develop any alignment in objectives and form a trust-based relationship.

Stakeholder theory

While agency theory and stewardship theory apply to the relationship between the owners and the executives, stakeholder theory applies to a broader societal perspective of corporate governance.

Stakeholder theory argues that an organization should recognize their responsibilities to all those affected by the organization's decisions, actions and behaviours. After all, an organization is not only an entity that creates value for its owners, but it also has obligations to society at large, to the state, to its employees, to its business partners in the supply chain, and to its customers.

Consequently, the theory argues that the directors be accountable to the extended stakeholders' group. Owning up to this responsibility is the price society demands from an incorporated organization which enjoys certain privileges such as limited liability for company debts and preferential allotment of natural resources.

The key challenge to stakeholder theory comes from defining the stakeholders for an organization. Including a wide range of interested parties may be well-intentioned and theoretically acceptable, but if the executives have to take everyone into consideration, they may not be able to create value for the owners. This may further result in chaos for the organization. In fact, firms in free-market economies have been reluctant to accept stakeholder theory due to their relatively narrow focus on firm growth.

Models of governance

Corporate governance models differ across geographies and much of the differences stem from the prevailing legal systems as applicable to companies. The three main models of governance, the Anglo-American model, the continental European model, and the Japanese model, are discussed in this section. In addition, we also discuss the governance model in family-owned businesses prevalent in many Asian countries, including India.

Anglo-American model

Companies in the US are subject to their respective state's company laws and corporate regulations where they are incorporated. However, investor protection, auditing requirements, and financial disclosures of public companies are federal responsibilities, primarily overseen by the Securities and Exchange Commission (SEC).

The basic governance model in the US is the unitary board (see Figure 2.1) with predominantly external independent directors. While the SEC and stock exchanges ensure the presence of audit, nomination and remuneration committees for the boards, shareholders have little influence on board

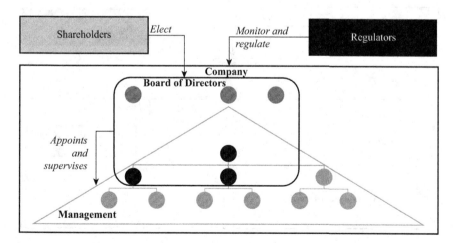

Figure 2.1 Unitary board structure

membership. There is also no mandatory segregation of roles between the chairperson and the CEO (Tricker and Tricker, 2015).

In the US, governance is regulated by legal statutes and regulations, where directors are held liable for non-compliance. This makes the governance model "rule-based".

The British / Commonwealth model has a lot in common with its American counterpart. As in the American model, company law in the British / Commonwealth model is based on common law, rooted in legislation, extended by case law.

The key difference with the American model is that the British / Commonwealth model is "principle-based", i.e. principles of corporate governance determine board responsibilities and the board only needs to explain how they have upheld the principles, making self-regulation the key theme.

Similar to the American model, corporate governance codes call for a high level of transparency and accountability, the presence of external independent directors, and audit, remuneration and nomination committees for the boards. However, the code also requires segregation of chairperson and CEO roles.

Continental European model

The continental European model of corporate governance promotes two-tier boards (see Figure 2.2) – the first one is the management board, constituted of internal executives, and the second one is the supervisory board, constituted of external directors and representatives of employees.

In continental European countries company laws are rule-based, developed on civil laws that consist of legally binding rules, which evolve further only through legislation.

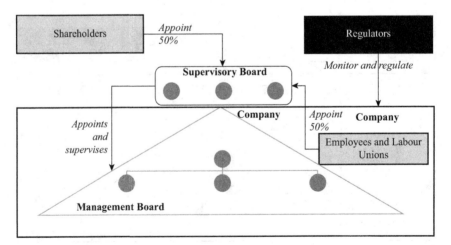

Figure 2.2 Two-tier board structure

The genesis of the two-tier board lies in the ownership structure of most European companies. Investors tend to be more concentrated, sometimes with dominant family shareholding. In addition, loans from banks and financial services companies are widely used to raise capital, and therefore these financial services organizations have greater control over the corporate affairs of the firms.

One of the criticisms of the two-tier model is that the management board, being totally internal in nature, may lack the external perspectives and knowledge that outside directors could bring to the table. On the other hand, the supervisory board may not be effective, due to lack of real control over the company, and the representative structure of the supervisory board promotes conflicts of interest.

Japanese model

Japanese companies follow the "keiretsu" model, where the boards are large, and mostly consist of the top bracket of the management team. The model is a reflection of the social cohesion within Japanese society, underlining consensus-based decision-making.

In this context, the presence of independent directors on the board is seen as unnecessary, as outsiders may never know enough about the company to contribute effectively.

The basic governance model in Japanese companies is carried out through a unitary board that consists of company executives. However, Japanese company law allows for independent outside directors, who may form advisory committees to the board.

The Japanese organizational communication approach encourages dialogue up and down the management hierarchy before arriving at an agreed position on any important decision. As a result, the board ends up ratifying decisions rather than making decisions.

Investors play limited roles in the corporate affairs of Japanese companies. However, since the early 21st century the traditional "keiretsu" model of relationship-based governance has been questioned, and some companies are adopting the American style governance model, with increased focus on shareholders' interests.

Family business model

A large number of firms in the Asian continent are owned and controlled by families. For example, overseas Chinese business people control a large number of firms in Singapore, Malaysia, Taiwan, Indonesia, etc. Similarly, "chaebol" groups in South Korea are controlled by the dominant owner-family interests. In India, family-oriented business groups maintain controlling stakes in several large companies promoted by these business groups.

These family-based companies attract outside capital, but the boards are essentially insider boards, ensuring the family's influence in all key decisions. Majority equity stake is kept within the family, distributed among family members and relatives, which enables entrepreneurial activities, where the paternalistic chairperson is supported by the family member directors. The company is seen as family wealth with additional support of the capital markets, and the custodians tend to believe in intuitive decision-making and hard bargaining with all stakeholders, sometimes with limited interest in scientific management principles.

Corporate governance, as practiced in the western world, is largely missing in these companies, as transparency is limited, accountability to external shareholders is absent, and fairness may not be present in all actions, with executive powers concentrated with the owner-directors.

References and further reading

Fernando, A. C. (2012). *Corporate Governance: Principles, Policies and Practices* (2nd edn). Chennai: Pearson Education India.

Monks, R. A. (2008). *Corpocracy: How CEOs and the Business Roundtable Hijacked the World's Greatest Wealth Machine – and How to Get it Back*. Hoboken, NJ: John Wiley & Sons.

Tricker, R. B., & Tricker, R. I. (2015). *Corporate Governance: Principles, Policies, and Practices* (3rd edn). Oxford: Oxford University Press.

3 Global benchmarks, reforms and initiatives in India

Introduction

While research about operations and motivations of joint-stock companies and agent-principal conflicts dates back to the 1930s (Berle and Means, 1932 in Daily, Dalton and Cannella, 2003, p. 372), development of policies and frameworks took place only in the latter part of the 20th century. The Cadbury Committee, which was set up in the early 1990s in the UK, formed the foundations of corporate governance policies not only in the UK but also in several other developed countries. The Cadbury Committee was followed by other committees on corporate governance, and their recommendations eventually shaped the guidelines and operating frameworks of corporate governance in the UK and other countries. The Sarbanes–Oxley Act in the US, post Enron scandal, was another landmark set of regulations that helped shape governance frameworks in many other countries, including India, especially in the areas of auditing.

In the past two decades Indian policymakers, institutions and industry bodies have worked extensively on developing standards, guidelines, and regulations on how companies in India would be operated and governed. The focus was to improve transparency, responsibility, accountability, and fairness in business operations. Referring to the available policies and frameworks of the developed countries as inputs, and taking into consideration unique elements of the business and industry landscape in India, various committees, under the aegis of different institutions and the Ministry of Corporate Affairs, have developed guidelines and regulations that are contributing to improving corporate governance standards in the country.

The Cadbury Committee on corporate governance, 1992

The Cadbury Committee was set up to

> help raise the standards of corporate governance and the level of confidence in financial reporting and auditing by setting out clearly what

it sees as the respective responsibilities of those involved and what it believes is expected of them. (Fernando, 2012)

The committee, based on its assessment of the accountability of board members to the shareholders and society at large, submitted its code of best practices, including 19 recommendations that stressed upon the board their role and the importance of following a set of best practices through self-regulation.

The Cadbury Committee's recommendations on boards of directors included meeting regularly, effective monitoring of the executive management, ensuring clear division of responsibilities to ensure balance of power, having non-executive directors with the right capabilities, establishing a formal schedule to deliberate on important decisions, forming procedures for seeking independent professional advice, and liaising with the company secretary on board procedures.

Specific recommendations for non-executive directors included bringing in independent judgment on matters of strategy, performance and resources, avoiding business or other relationships with the management, having appointments for a specific duration, with selection of the non-executive directors occurring through a formal process.

For executive directors, the Cadbury Committee recommended that directors' service contracts beyond three years must have shareholders' approval, full and clear disclosure of total emoluments, with executive directors' pay decided on by a remuneration committee.

The Cadbury Committee's recommendations on reporting and control also mentioned the board's responsibility to present a balanced and understandable assessment of the company's position, maintaining a professional relationship with the auditors, formation of an audit committee with clear terms of reference, taking responsibility for the company's system of internal controls, and owning the responsibility of reporting on the business as a going concern (Fernando, 2012).

Combined Code, 1998

In order to address concerns associated with the Cadbury Committee recommendations, the Paul Ruthman Committee, the Greenbury Committee and the Hampel Committee were set up in the following years to fine-tune therecommendations of the Cadbury Committee (Fernando, 2012).

The Combined Code of 1998 was derived from the recommendations of these committees and became a part of the listing rules of the London Stock Exchange. Some specific additions in the Combined Code included directors' responsibility to review the effectiveness of the system of internal controls that cover financial, operational, compliance, and risk management, and report the same to the shareholders (Code, 1998). In addition, it also included the

Greenbury Committee's recommendation on remuneration committees of the board and remuneration policy, which was that remuneration committees should consist of independent non-executive directors only.

Sarbanes–Oxley Act, 2002

The Sarbanes–Oxley Act (SOX) was enacted in a flurry of US congressional activity after the spectacular failures of the once highly regarded firms Enron and WorldCom (Romano, 2004). Officially known as the Public Company Accounting Reform and Investor Protection Act of 2002, SOX was designed to rectify auditing issues among publicly listed companies in the US. SOX created a unique, quasi-public institution, the Public Company Accounting Oversight Board (PCAOB), to oversee and regulate auditing by enlisting auditors who would enforce existing laws against theft and fraud by corporate officers. In addition, new provisions were created to address the concerns related to the auditor-firm relationship, auditor rotation, auditor provision of non-audit services, and corporate whistle-blowers. Thus, while company boards reported to the Securities and Exchange Commission (SEC), auditors would report to the PCAOB.

Specifically, SOX brought in an improved audit committee, consisting of independent directors who would be responsible for the appointment of, and the work of, the auditors. In addition, it addressed conflicts of interest between the company executives and the auditors, rotation of auditors, and the prohibition of performing non-audit services by the auditors.

Apart from focusing on improving audit activities, SOX also insisted that the CEO and CFO of an organization certify reports filed with the SEC, and that they must take responsibility for restating financial statements, establishing limitations on loans to the directors, fixing responsibilities of company attorneys, and articulating expectations from the securities analysts. Any wrongdoings would attract stiff penalties.

The purpose of SOX was to enhance accountability for all players – from the directors to the security analysts – involved in the financials of a publicly listed organization in the US, making it clear that these individuals are responsible for improved governance and restoring investor confidence.

OECD Principles, 1999, 2002 and 2015

The OECD Principles of Corporate Governance, initially issued in 1999 to address growing corporate governance failures in developed countries, were revised in 2004 to reflect on the experiences of emerging and developing economies (Jesover and Kirkpatrick, 2005). Subsequently, the principles were reviewed in 2015, to take into consideration the changes in the business environment, and ensure the better functioning of financial markets (OECD, 2015). The six principles of corporate governance, as articulated by the OECD, are as follows:

I   Ensuring the basis for an effective corporate governance framework

The corporate governance framework should promote transparent and fair markets, and the efficient allocation of resources. It should be consistent with the rule of law and support effective supervision and enforcement.

II   The rights and equitable treatment of shareholders and key ownership functions

The corporate governance framework should protect and facilitate the exercise of shareholders' rights and ensure the equitable treatment of all shareholders, including minority and foreign shareholders. All shareholders should have the opportunity to obtain effective redress for violation of their rights.

III   Institutional investors, stock markets, and other intermediaries

The corporate governance framework should provide sound incentives throughout the investment chain and provide for stock markets to function in a way that contributes to good corporate governance.

IV   The role of stakeholders in corporate governance

The corporate governance framework should recognise the rights of stakeholders established by law or through mutual agreements and encourage active co-operation between corporations and stakeholders in creating wealth, jobs, and the sustainability of financially sound enterprises.

V   Disclosure and transparency

The corporate governance framework should ensure that timely and accurate disclosure is made on all material matters regarding the corporation, including the financial situation, performance, ownership, and governance of the company.

VI   The responsibilities of the board

The corporate governance framework should ensure the strategic guidance of the company, the effective monitoring of management by the board, and the board's accountability to the company and the shareholders. (OECD, 2015)

In short, the first principle emphasizes the importance of the corporate governance framework in promoting transparent and fair markets, and allocating resources efficiently. The second principle outlines shareholder rights, including the right to information and participation in key company decisions. The third principle recognizes the need for sound economic incentives throughout the investment chain, with a particular focus on institutional investors. The fourth principle identifies the benefits of cooperation between corporations and their respective stakeholders. The fifth principle identifies the areas of disclosure, such as financial and operating results, company goals and objectives, ownership of stakes, remuneration, related party transactions, risk factors, board composition, and key non-financial information. The sixth principle provides guidance on the key functions of the board of directors, including how they are expected to review corporate strategy, selecting and compensating management, overseeing major corporate restructuring activities, and ensuring the integrity of the corporation's accounting and financial reporting systems. In addition, this principle also recommends board training and evaluation and establishment of specialized board committees in areas such as remuneration, audit and risk management. The OECD principles are non-binding and are considered to be the international reference point for corporate governance.

SEBI initiatives

The Securities Exchange Board of India (SEBI) is the regulatory authority that protects the interests of investors in securities and promotes the development and regulation of the securities market in India, and other associated activities. As of 2017, with over 5000 listed companies, India accounted for nearly 2.5 per cent of global stock market capitalization (SEBI, 2017). Corporate India, representing a vibrant mix of small and large companies, with a similarly diverse mix of large institutional investors and small retail investors, is a key driver in the nation's development. Promoting superior corporate governance practices in listed companies, creating appropriate binding regulations and non-binding recommendations, and bringing in systematic reforms are part of SEBI's charter.

One of the first attempts in developing a formal governance code for corporations in India was made by the Confederation of Indian Industries (CII) in 1998. However, CII's Desirable Code of Corporate Governance, which recommended adopting many international best practices for Indian organizations, were not binding on the organizations, and therefore adoption was voluntary and sparse (Sarkar and Sarkar, 2012). Around the same time, SEBI saw the need for statutory governance codes due to malpractices in the stock market, insider trading, incorrect valuation etc. In this context, SEBI instituted the Kumar Mangalam Birla Committee on Corporate Governance, to formalize measures for improving corporate governance practices in companies listed in Indian stock markets.

Kumar Mangalam Birla Committee recommendations, 2000

The KM Birla Committee's mandatory recommendations applied to all listed companies with paid-up capital of INR 30 million or above. It recommended that the board must have an optimum combination of executive and non-executive directors. The committee also recommended a qualified and independent audit committee to enhance financial disclosure and promote transparency. The remuneration committee of the board must decide the remuneration of non-executive directors, and the company must fully disclose remuneration packages for all the directors. The KM Birla Committee also mandated at least four meetings of the board per year and defined board procedures. In addition, the Directors' Report, published as part of the annual report, must contain information about the industry, competitive landscape, operating performance, business risks and internal control systems. The committee also insisted on improving direct communication to shareholders (GoI, 2000).

In addition, the non-mandatory recommendations of the committee included segregation between the CEO / MD and the chairperson, shareholders' rights to financial performance information of the company, and voting on key issues through postal ballot.

The committee's report was accepted and implemented through listing requirements in stock exchanges through a new clause, Clause 49.

Narayana Murthy Committee recommendations, 2003

As corporate governance practices kept evolving, with a series of compliance reports and disclosures arriving from listed companies, SEBI wanted to evolve and strengthen its code of governance. Towards this end, SEBI initiated the Narayana Murthy Committee, which submitted its recommendations in 2003.

The Narayana Murthy Committee made several mandatory recommendations on the operating procedures of the audit committee, related party transactions, dealing with proceeds from IPO, managing risks, and adopting a code of conduct for the board members, compensation to the non-executive directors, and institutionalizing whistle-blower policy in the company (GoI, 2003).

The committee's recommendations were actioned by SEBI with the revision of Clause 49 in 2004. Important changes included definition of independent directors, responsibility and powers of the audit committee, enhanced disclosures on accounting treatments, related party transactions (RPTs), and CEO / CFO certification of the statement of accounts (Sarkar and Sarkar, 2012).

Uday Kotak Committee recommendations, 2017

In 2017, the Uday Kotak Committee submitted its recommendations to SEBI on improving standards of corporate governance in listed companies in India. The committee made newer recommendations with respect to composition and role of the board, like a minimum of six directors in a listed company, one independent female director, directors' presence in other boards to be capped to seven, the CEO / MD must not be related to the chairperson, and mandatory disclosure of expertise of the directors. In addition, the committee insisted on excluding board-interlocks, i.e., an independent director and a non-independent director in one company could not be allowed to play reverse roles in another company. The recommendations also included enhancement of functioning of board committees, monitoring group entities, mandatory quarterly financial disclosure, disclosures on board evaluation and action taken, and disclosure of the medium and long-term strategies of the company (SEBI, 2017).

It is interesting to note that some of these stringent recommendations – such as at least one independent director must be a woman – have been questioned by the Ministry of Corporate Affairs, highlighting the importance of the "ease of doing business" in India.

Clause 49 of SEBI's Listing Obligations and Disclosure Requirements (LODR) has undergone periodic revisions to address the changing business environment, company laws and SEBI's own committee recommendations, including the Uday Kotak Committee's recommendations. The latest provisions of Clause 49 can be found on their website (SEBI 2019).

Initiatives of the Ministry of Corporate of Affairs

While SEBI was updating Clause 49 of the Listing Agreement, the then Department of Corporate Affairs set up the Naresh Chandra Committee to analyse and recommend changes to the issues related to the statutory auditor-company relationship, certification of accounts and financial statements by the management and the directors, and the role of independent directors (Sarkar and Sarkar, 2012).

Naresh Chandra Committee recommendations, 2002

Taking cue from the SOX Act in the US, the Naresh Chandra Committee brought in strict guidelines defining relationships between auditors and their clients, along with a list of prohibited non-audit services for audit firms. The committee also recommended certain immunities to independent directors to rope in competent people to the boards of Indian companies (Fernando, 2012).

JJ Irani Committee recommendations, 2005

In 2004, the government of India formed the JJ Irani Committee to review aspects of the Companies Act 1956 to make it compact, remove ambiguity, and at the same time provide for flexibility to cater to the evolving business models of Indian companies.

The committee's recommendations were at odds with SEBI's Listing Agreement regarding the proportion of independent directors a board should have. The committee also proposed a pyramidal structure of corporates, where a subsidiary company could by itself become a holding company. In addition, the committee empowered shareholders in making certain decisions, recommended self-regulation, and at the same time stringent penalties for violations (MCA, 2005).

Based on these recommendations, the Ministry of Corporate Affairs introduced the Companies Bill 2009 with the intent to revise and modify the Companies Act 1956. At a later point this was withdrawn and a modified version, the Companies Bill 2011, was introduced to lawmakers. This bill eventually was approved to become the new Companies Act 2013.

Companies Act 2013

The Companies Act 1956 had several outdated provisions and thus needed a thorough overhaul. The Companies Act 2013 (CA2013) was expected to significantly change the manner in which corporates operate in India. The provisions of CA2013 specifically included provisions for the composition of board of directors, diversity of the board, independence of the independent directors with no pecuniary relationship with management, presence of a resident director, and liability of independent directors' acts of negligence. In addition, it recommends at least four board-level committees – an audit committee, nomination and remuneration committee, stakeholder relationship / investor grievance committee, and CSR committee. With regard to board meetings and processes, CA2013 provided process-level details, and also allowed for participation in board meetings by video conference.

While in-depth discussion of CA2013 is beyond the scope of the book, we will set out the key provisions of CA2013 under six themes: (a) enhanced reporting framework; (b) increased auditor accountability; (c) improved restructuring; (d) emphasis on investor protection; (e) greater responsibilities for directors and management; and (f) inclusive CSR agenda (MCA, 2013). Salient points under each theme are mentioned below.

(a) Enhanced reporting framework:

- New definition of subsidiary, associate, and joint-venture companies.
- Mandatory requirement for consolidated financial statement.
- Mandatory internal audit and reporting on internal financial controls.

(b) Increased auditor accountability:

- Clause on auditor appointment and rotation.
- Defined auditor reporting responsibilities.

(c) Improved restructuring:

- Rationalizing multi-layered structures.
- Simplifying procedures for mergers.
- Restrictions in buybacks.

(d) Emphasis on investor protection:

- Clause on related party transactions.
- Clause on insider trading.
- Clause on fraud risk mitigation.

(e) Greater responsibilities for directors and management:

- Additional responsibility of independent directors.
- Clause on audit committee composition and responsibilities.
- Defined structure and content of directors' report.

(f) Inclusive CSR agenda:

- Obligation triggers and computation of expected CSR spend.
- Administration and reporting of CSR activities.

CA2013 has undergone several amendments in the past few years. While many of these amendments relate to fine-tuning the legalese for appropriate implementation, some amendments relate to significant changes in corporate governance practices. For example, an ordinance in 2018 deliberated on remuneration of the directors, and it removed the provision of remuneration of independent directors, who could only be compensated with either commission, reimbursement of expenses made for the company, indemnity or other services including sitting fees. Similarly, as per the ordinance, a person would not be able to be a director of more than 20 companies, and any default contravening the provision would lead to termination of directorship.

Conclusion

Just as global benchmarks and standards on corporate governance have evolved and strengthened over time, we observe that in India similar initiatives have been undertaken over the past two decades to improve corporate governance standards. The largest regulatory changes in India have been as a result of CA2013, applicable to all companies, and Clause 49 of SEBI's LODR, applicable to listed companies. CA2013 might have come as a response to the large-scale accounting fraud discovered at Satyam Computer Services. In the next part of this book we will see how Indian companies have evolved in their governance parameters and how the changes contributed to their performance.

References and further reading

Code, C. (1998). *Combined Code, Principles of Corporate Governance*. London: Gee & Co. Ltd.

Daily, C. M., Dalton, D. R., & Cannella Jr, A. A. (2003). Corporate governance: Decades of dialogue and data. *Academy of Management Review*, 28(3), 371–382.

Fernando, A. C. (2012). *Corporate Governance: Principles, Policies and Practices*. Chennai: Pearson Education India.

GoI (2000). *Kumar Mangalam Committee Report*. Government of India. Available at https://archive.india.gov.in/business/corporate_governance/kumarmangalam.php. Last accessed 7 April 2019.

GoI (2003). *Narayana Murthy Committee Report*. Government of India. Available at https://archive.india.gov.in/business/corporate_governance/narayana_murthy.php. Last accessed 7 April 2019.

Jesover, F., & Kirkpatrick, G. (2005). The revised OECD principles of corporate governance and their relevance to non-OECD countries. *Corporate Governance: An International Review*, 13(2), 127–136.

MCA (2005). *Report of the Expert Committee on the Company Law: JJ Irani Committee Report, Ministry of Corporate Affairs*. Available at http://reports.mca.gov.in/Reports/23-Irani%20committee%20report%20of%20the%20expert%20committee%20on%20Company%20law,2005.pdf. Last accessed 7 April 2019.

MCA (2013). *The Companies Act 2013*. Ministry of Corporate Affairs. Available at www.mca.gov.in/Ministry/pdf/CompaniesAct2013.pdf. Last accessed 7 April 2019.

OECD (2015). *G20/OECD Principles of Corporate Governance*. Paris: OECD Publishing. https://doi.org/10.1787/9789264236882-en. Last accessed 7 April 2019.

Romano, R. (2004). The Sarbanes–Oxley Act and the making of quack corporate governance. *Yale Law Journal*, 114(7), 1521–1611.

Sarkar, J., & Sarkar, S. (2012). *Corporate Governance in India*. New Delhi: SAGE Publishing.

SEBI (2017). *Uday Kotak Committee Recommendations on Corporate Governance*. Securities Exchange Board of India. Available at www.sebi.gov.in/reports/reports/oct-2017/report-of-the-committee-on-corporate-governance_36177.html. Last accessed 7 April 2019.

SEBI (2019). *SEBI (Listing Obligations and Disclosure Requirements) Regulations 2015* (Last amended on March 29, 2019). Available at www.sebi.gov.in/legal/regulations/feb-2017/sebi-listing-obligations-and-disclosure-requirements-regulations-2015-last-amended-on-march-29-2019-_37269.html. Last accessed 7 April 2019.

Part II
Empirical evidence from India

4 Members of the board

Composition, contribution and compensation

Case: Satyam Computers

In September 2008, Satyam Computer Services Ltd., a Hyderabad-based IT services organization, received the Golden Peacock Award for Excellence in Corporate Governance from the World Council for Corporate Governance. Around the same time the company's board was deliberating on the decision to invest about INR 70 billion in Maytas Properties and Maytas Infrastructure – two companies promoted and controlled by the founder of Satyam, Mr. Ramalinga Raju.

On December 16, 2008, Satyam's board approved the investment. At that time Satyam was one of the most favoured stocks in the market, with its market capitalization hovering around INR 152.62 billion. The decision to acquire the two companies was agreed upon by all six independent directors and one executive director. The two promoter directors did not vote as they were interested parties. The board of Satyam at that time included Ramalinga Raju (founder and CEO), B. Rama Raju (Ramalinga Raju's brother and co-founder), Vinod Dham (venture capitalist, ex-Intel executive and inventor of Pentium), Krishna Palepu (professor of finance, control and strategy at Harvard Business School), Mangalam Srinivasan (retired professor from many US universities, including UC, Berkeley), T.R. Prasad (former cabinet secretary of the Government of India), Rammohan Rao (dean of the Indian School of Business), U.S. Raju (former director of the Indian Institute of Technology, Delhi), and Ram Mynampati (full-time executive with rich professional experience, and the president of the company). Needless to say, this was probably one of the most illustrious set of independent directors an Indian company had on their board at that time. Records from the company's annual reports for fiscal 2007–2008 showed that the independent directors were compensated handsomely too. One might wonder how the independent directors chose to agree to the founder's proposal to buy unrelated companies owned by founder's family while the company could deploy funds more effectively elsewhere. And indeed, in this case, the board's decision to acquire the unrelated businesses of the promoter's family did not go well with the investors, and on their strong protest, the board had to retract the decision to acquire. Consequently, some independent directors resigned from their board positions.

Subsequently, on January 7, 2009, Ramalinga Raju, founder and CEO of Satyam Computers, announced that his company had been falsifying its accounts for years, overstating revenues and inflating profits.

Resigning as Satyam's chairman and CEO, Raju said in a letter addressed to his board, the stock exchanges, and the market regulator – the Securities & Exchange Board of India (SEBI) – that Satyam's profits were inflated over several years to "unmanageable proportions" and that it was forced to carry more assets and resources than its real operations justified. Taking sole responsibility for these acts, he further stated that "it was like riding a tiger, not knowing how to get off without being eaten" (www.outlookindia.com/website/story/it-was-like-riding-a-tiger/239402). In his communication Raju acknowledged that Satyam's balance sheet included INR 71.36 billion in non-existent cash and bank balances, accrued interest and misstatements. It had also inflated its 2008 second quarter revenues by INR 5.88 billion, and the true operating margin was less than a tenth of the stated value. The company's fixed deposits documents were forged too. The real number of employees was about 40,000 while the documents showed the number was 53,000.

The Satyam episode was tragic and it had international ramifications. At that time Satyam served as the back office of some of the largest banks, manufacturers, healthcare and media companies in the world, handling everything from computer systems to customer service. Clients included General Electric, General Motors, Nestlé and the US government. In some cases, Satyam was even responsible for clients' finances and accounting. Investors in the US immediately initiated two class-action suits against the company for its American Depository Receipts (ADRs). Uncertainty surrounded the survival of the company. Customers were reassessing their contracts, and employees were in a state of shock. The world knew that India was perennially weak in the implementation of regulations, but no one expected such a revelation from a company that was given The Golden Peacock award barely four months previously! On January 9, 2009 Satyam's market capitalization fell by about 90% of what it had been three weeks ago, to INR 16.07 billion, amid large-scale selling in the stock-market. It was also interesting to note that, according to the data filed with the regulators, the promoter's stake in the company reduced from 25.60 per cent at the end of fiscal 2001 to 2.18 per cent at the end of fiscal 2008. At the time of the scandal, foreign institutional investors and American Depository shareholders held a more than 60 per cent stake in the company.

The government and regulators responded with some swift action of damage control. On January 9, 2009, the board of the company was superseded by 10 nominee directors from the government. Regulators initiated investigations and promised appropriate penal action against those who were found guilty.

Even the common people, those who did not directly deal in the stock market or who did not have direct interest in the discourse of corporate governance, were bewildered by the magnitude and scope of this corporate fraud. Many questioned the roles played by the highly competent and well-paid board, and particularly the independent directors. However, some were sympathetic towards the independent directors – after all, how could they scrutinize every operational detail?

The Satyam episode brought to light the weak link in the prevailing corporate governance structure – the independent directors. They were supposed to bring objectivity to the oversight function of the board and improve its effectiveness, but at Satyam they could not deliver on their fiduciary duties of protecting the interest of shareholders and the company.

Importance of boards in effective corporate governance

The primary characteristics of effective corporate governance include transparency, management oversight and control, protection of the rights of all shareholders, and directors' involvement in independently reviewing and approving the corporation's strategy and major business plans and decisions. These factors are expected to contribute positively towards maximization of shareholder value through superior and sustained firm performance and value creation. The board of directors is expected to act on behalf of the shareholders, and provide guidance and directions to the executive management team. The board is directly accountable to the shareholders to ensure the company's prosperity. In addition to business and financial decisions, the board is also expected to deal with issues related to other governance issues, corporate social responsibility and corporate ethics (IICA, 2015).

However, in the past two decades we have observed a series of large-scale corporate scandals, frauds and failures across the globe – from Enron and WorldCom in the US, to Parmalat in Italy, Sanlu in China, and Satyam Computers in India, causing significant losses to shareholders of these companies. Charan (2011) argues that in the wake of the implementation of the Sarbanes–Oxley act in the early 2000s, boards in the US have moved from being "ceremonial boards" that nod to their CEO's decisions to "liberated boards", i.e. the boards that are liberated from the CEO's dictums, and ask questions. Continuing further, some boards are moving towards becoming "progressive boards", who not only ask questions but also chart roadmaps for their companies, rely on group dynamics within the board, leverage information and focus on substantive issues (Charan, 2011). While developed countries like US have taken effective steps to improve the corporate governance standards and prevent such failures in the future, similar initiatives in India or other developing countries are only gaining ground now (Prasad, 2014).

Conceptual foundations and theoretical perspectives

Corporate governance is defined as the set of systems and processes by which companies are directed and controlled with the purpose of aligning the interest of individuals, corporations, and society as much as possible (Cadbury, 2000; Gregory, 2000). The need for corporate governance arises, in professionally managed listed companies, from the tension between the rights of shareholders and the operational control exercised by the management of the company. The principles of good corporate governance involve accountability, transparency, effectiveness, remuneration, relationship with shareholders, probity and focus on the sustainable success of an equity over the longer term. The OECD principles of good corporate governance, as discussed in Chapter 3, comprise the following elements: (a) alignment with the legal and regulatory requirements, (b) protection and facilitation of shareholders' rights, (c) equitable treatment of shareholders, and (d) disclosure and transparency of financial and operational information (OECD, 1999). Thus, the board has an important role and fiduciary duty to ensure these principles are held appropriately in the firm, both in spirit and practice.

While it might be argued that directors of the board would act rationally, making board-level decisions through an analytical process of carefully considering alternatives, the reality in most boards is different. Tricker and Tricker (2015) find that directors' behaviours are influenced by interpersonal relationships, by perceptions of positions, and by the processes of power, making corporate governance more of an organizational behaviour subject.

Stakeholder theory, which attempts to align the interests of managers and all, has been a subject of some investigation. John and Senbet (1998) conducted a detailed study of corporate governance through the concept of stakeholder theory. They note the presence of many parties interested in the well-being of the firm, with many of them often holding competing interests. Shareholders might welcome investments in high-yielding, but volatile, projects. However, such investments might jeopardize the interests of debt holders, especially when the firm is teetering on the edge of bankruptcy. The study also emphasizes the absence of a free-market system, citing as an example the need to determine an optimal size for the board of directors, especially in view of the tendency for board size to exhibit a negative correlation with firm performance. Other non-market mechanisms reviewed by John and Senbet (1998) include the need for designing a committee structure in a way that allows the setting-up of specialized committees for each critical area of operations, staffed by board members with specific expertise. Such a structure would allow, for instance, both productivity-oriented and monitoring-oriented committees.

The multiplicity of stakeholders as enshrined in stakeholder theory was highlighted by Jensen (2001), who concurred with John and Senbet (1998) that certain actions by the management might have conflicting effects on various classes of stakeholders. This implies that the managers have numerous objective functions to maximize firm performance, something that Jensen sees as an important drawback of the stakeholder theory as it violates the proposition that a single-valued objective is a prerequisite for purposeful or rational behaviour by any organization.

Jensen (2001) formulated the enlightened stakeholder theory in order to bring to the fore the single-valued objective function that conforms to rationality. The enlightened stakeholder theory provides that managers should pursue the maximization of the long-term value of the firm. This is with the view to protecting the interests of any major stakeholder, the violation of which leads to truncation of the objective of the firm's long-term value maximization.

Empirical analysis – research questions

In the context of the above-mentioned constructs, we now frame our research questions around the effectiveness of corporate boards in ensuring the interests of companies' stakeholders and long-term value creation. We analyse how factors such as composition of the board, contribution of board members in company's activities, directors' presence in other boards, CEO duality, and board compensation contribute to firms' profitability, market capitalization and returns to the shareholders.

Composition of the board and diversity of board members

It is the board's responsibility to ensure good governance and composition of an effective board needs to ensure the following factors.

Optimum size: While a small-sized board may expect members to be more involved in decision-making and setting the directions right, a large board may be able to bring in experts required to deal with complex business issues.

Independence: A board that consists of fewer insiders and more independent directors will become more proactive in making leadership decisions and may not suffer from agency issues.

Diversity: Varied experience, expertise, and professional qualifications of its directors, coupled with differences in cultural and ethnic backgrounds, make a board a multi-faceted entity with interwoven analytical processes, which potentially leads to more nuanced decisions.

Access to information: Effectiveness and efficiency of a board depends on timely, appropriate, accurate information.

Longer-term perspective: While CEOs may be focused on the immediate financial results of the company, the board should have a longer vision and broader responsibility for all stakeholders.

Thus, effectiveness of a board can be measured through indicators such as the presence of independent directors on the board, the presence of female directors on the board, directors' presence on other companies' boards, the presence of promoters on the board, and board members' professional and educational background.

Board size

Boards are considered to be important decision-making groups, and size can affect the decision-making process and effectiveness of the board (Dwivedi & Jain, 2005). Yermack (1996) has shown that there is an inverse association between board size and firm value, and companies with small boards tend to exhibit favourable values for financial ratios and provide stronger CEO performance. It is argued that if the size of the board is big, it might lead to the dilution of responsibilities, and individual board members might not be able to display their potential among the large crowd of board members. However, some researchers believe that a larger board may also bring in additional diversity in the board functions, which becomes more relevant in today's dynamic business environment (Dalton et al., 1998; Pearce & Zahra, 1992). In addition, a larger board size may create greater connections and links and hence provide access to more resources, while smaller boards have inadequate recognition of the need to initiate or support strategic change, a lack of clear understanding of alternatives, and / or a lack of confidence in recommending strategic change (Goilden & Zajac, 2001). Therefore, it is possible that an inverted "U" relationship exists, whereby the addition of directors adds to the skills mix and performance of the board and firm, till it reaches a point where the adverse dynamics of a large board outweigh the additional benefits of a greater skills mix, as suggested by Jensen (1993).

Nonetheless, increasing the size of the board by number does not necessarily promote diversity in the board, which is the real necessity for companies. In addition, our review of data on Indian corporations shows that there is significant variation in board sizes and there is little correlation between company size and board size. Therefore, we avoid considering absolute size of the board as a parameter for our analysis and explore other board composition parameters.

Presence of promoters in the board

Due to historical reasons many organizations in India have a significant number of promoters present on the board. Promoters and their family members often hold several director positions on the board, ignoring the necessity for professional directors. Such an approach ensures that promoters' interests are given maximum importance in board decisions. However, it has been observed that the promoters who do not bring in diversity to the board may not be effective in creating value for shareholders (Carter, Simkins & Simpson, 2003). Observing the director lists of large companies in India we notice that family members of the promoters who become directors bring in negligible diversity to the board.

Presence of independent directors

Independent directors are professionals who can easily achieve the supervising function, reduce the possibility of collusion of top executives, and prevent the abuse of company resources (Chiang & Chia, 2005). The stewardship theory suggests that superior corporate performance is linked to a majority of inside directors as they work to maximize profit for shareholders (Donaldson & Davis, 1991; Donaldson, 1990). Contrary to this, the agency theory suggests that a greater proportion of outside directors will be able to monitor any self-interested actions by managers and so will minimize the agency costs (Fama & Jensen, 1983; Fama, 1980).

Independent directors are expected to offer independent judgment on issues related to strategy, performance, and key appointments, and take an objective view on the performance evaluation of the board. Key decisions on certain topics should be passed only if a majority of the independent directors on the board votes in support of the decision. An independent director should be appointed for a specific duration during which he/she can be removed from his/her position only on specific grounds and after following due process (Balasubramanian, 2010).

Presence of female directors

The performance of a company is affected by the presence of heterogeneity across various organization levels, including the board level. Like managerial diversity, board diversity through the presence of female directors is an important element of organizational behaviour research. It is argued that female directors bring unique and valuable resources and relationships to their boards with their diverse experience, knowledge, observational and perceptive strengths (Smith, Smith & Verner, 2006).

Therefore, in this study we measure board composition by the combined factors of the presence of independent directors, female directors, and promoters on the board. We posit that diversity in board composition positively influences firm performance.

Contribution and involvement of board members

Research shows that the involvement of board members in a firm's activities varies widely. While minute tracking of the company's operational activities is undesirable, it is expected that directors leverage their experience, knowledge and judgment to guide the company towards achieving its objectives. We look at two sub-factors – participation in board meetings and presence in board committees – as measures for board members' involvement.

Directors' participation in board meetings

Interactions among directors in board meetings help improve the effectiveness of boards (Conger, Finegold & Lawler, 1998). Lipton and Lorsch (1992) suggest that greater frequency of board meetings is likely to result in superior performance. Attendance at board meetings is the main channel through which directors get the information required to carry out their duties. Lack of attendance at board meetings may lead directors to give improper advice related to the strategy of the firm, and they will be ineffective at monitoring and guiding the management.

Directors' presence in board committees

The presence of directors in different board committees can help them to monitor of the different management activities of the firm. Committees can benefit from the presence of several directors, as they will get expert advice on the various aspects of governance. This leads us to take a deep dive into the "busyness hypothesis" (Ferris, Jagannathan & Pritchard, 2003). Some studies have reported that directors with multiple appointments have a positive impact on firm performance (Ferris et al., 2003; Harris & Shimizu, 2004; Miwa & Ramseyer, 2000). However, it is often argued that too many appointments for directors can lead to over-commitment, thereby reducing their ability to have a keen focus on matters related to company management.

Thus, board members' involvement in firm's activities is measured through two sub-factors, attendance in board meetings and presence of directors in committees, and we posit that focus and attention from directors on firm operations positively influences firm performance.

Directors' presence in other boards

When a director is also a director in a few other companies, they get rich exposure to board-level issues, opportunities, and challenges. This helps them leverage cross-learning, and discharge their responsibilities as a director more effectively. As per resource dependence theory, outside directors provide access to resources needed by the firm. For example, outside directors who are also executives of financial institutions may assist in securing favourable lines of credit (Daily, Dalton & Cannella, 2003). However, at the same time, the director may not have sufficient time to deep-dive into the problems of any one of the companies.

Therefore, as a director starts participating in multiple boards, his / her effectiveness improves and with further participation in more boards, the effectiveness deteriorates. Therefore, we posit, directors' presence in other boards has an inverted-U relationship with the effectiveness of the directors.

CEO duality

Duality refers to a board leadership structure in which one person fulfils the role of both the chairperson of the board and the CEO / managing director. Previous studies have debated CEO duality: one group believes that it leads to superior performance of the firm, as the CEO gets the right to clear-cut leadership for the purposes of strategy formulation and implementation (Anderson & Anthony, 1986). The other group of people argues that duality leads to less effective leadership, as it would reduce the independence of the board. It is also argued that in the case of duality there is a chance that a rivalry is created between the chairperson and the CEO. There might be confusion, as the company would have two spokespeople, and the leadership might be diluted. According to agency theory, an agency problem exists when an agent has established goals which conflict with those of the principal. Likewise, in working as a chairperson, the CEO is bound to get more power and this might weaken the control of the board over the firm.

History has shown that duality has often resulted in a decline in performance, with firm such as Westinghouse, Sears, General Motors, and IBM (White & Ingrassia, 1992). Likewise, the non-duality of Compaq Computers is referenced as a reason for its success. Therefore, we posit, CEO duality negatively influences firm performance.

Compensation to board members

Trend data from Indian corporates suggests that past government interventions placed limitations on corporate sector pay in India, and that such unrealistic interventions led to off-the-record methods for compensating executive directors. Fortunately, the scenario has changed for the better, and now remuneration packages of directors must be individually approved at a general meeting of shareholders (Balasubramanian, 2010).

Managerial compensation typically has two components – salary and performance-based commission – as well as retirement and other benefits and prerequisites. An analysis of around 300 Indian firms suggests that the average total compensation of Indian CEOs rose almost threefold between 1998 and 2004 (Chakrabarti, Megginson & Yadav, 2008). During this period, the proportion of profit-based commission rose steadily, and the proportion of CEOs with commission as part of their pay package rose from 13.4 per cent to 25.6 per cent. CEO pay has thus clearly become more performance-based over the past few decades.

The executive compensation literature (Murphy, 1999; Zhu, Tian & Ma, 2009) suggests that compensation should be related to measures of stock-based performance, not only because this is desired by shareholders, but also because high stock returns should signal positive information on the actions taken by managers. It is advised that the remuneration committee take full control of the remuneration process, policies, and practices. In particular, remuneration committees should jealously guard their initiation rights over executive remuneration (Balasubramanian, 2010). On the other hand, board members' compensation can be an important motivating factor for them to get involved in improving the company's performance. Thus, we posit, board compensation positively influences firm performance.

Data and methodology

We have chosen 200 companies from India, listed in the National Stock Exchange's (NSE) Nifty200 index, for this study and analysed these companies' board activities and performance over the fiscal years 1999–2018. The companies represent a wide range of sectors, from primary industries such as agriculture and mining, to secondary and tertiary industries such as manufacturing, banking, retail and information technology. The Centre for Monitoring Indian Economy's (CMIE) Prowess database and annual reports from the companies have been used to retrieve all firm-level information, i.e. financial performance, stock market performance, ownership data, and board-level information. This unbalanced panel data has 3,141 company-year records. Multivariate regression has been used to analyse the data with separate multiple regression models for each dependent variable.

The variables used for multivariate regression are listed in Table 4.1. We have chosen 13 dependent variables, viz. return on net worth; return on total assets; return on capital employed; net profit margin; profit before depreciation, interest, tax and amortization (PBDITA) as a percentage of sales; annual revenue growth; major corporate restructuring reported; dividend rate; dividend yield; Tobin's Q; ratio of market capitalization and enterprise value; Jensen's alpha; and CAPM's beta, to represent diverse aspects of firm performance. While the first five measures represent the financial performance of the firm, the next two represent the business performance of the firm, and the remaining six represent performance from market and shareholders' perspectives, i.e. how the market perceives the future value of the firm, and the returns shareholders get from the firm.

A range of corporate governance factors have been used as independent variables to assess our research questions. Board composition is measured through size of the board; number of female directors; CEO duality; number of executive directors; number of promoter directors; number of independent directors; and directors' presence in other companies' boards. CEO duality is computed based on whether for a given financial year, the CEO / MD was also the chairperson of the board. Contribution of board members is measured through directors' presence in board meetings and directors' presence in board committees. Compensations of the board members is measured through the average of total directors' remuneration. These parameters are defined in Table 4.2.

Table 4.1 Variable definitions – dependent variables

Variable	Type	Unit and data type	Definition / formula / explanation
Return on net worth (%)	Dependent	Numeric, percentage	Measures profitability of a company for a financial year, taking shareholders' equity as the basis. It is calculated as net income / shareholders' equity.
Return on total assets (%)	Dependent	Numeric, percentage	Measures profitability of a company for a financial year, taking total assets of the firm as the basis. It is calculated as profit before depreciation, interest, tax and amortization (PBDITA) / total assets.
Return on capital employed (%)	Dependent	Numeric, percentage	Measures a company's profitability and the efficiency with which its capital is employed. ROCE is calculated as PBDITA / capital employed.
Net profit margin (%)	Dependent	Numeric, percentage	Measures profitability of a company for a financial year, taking total revenue as the basis. It is calculated as net income / total revenue.
PBDITA as % of total income (%)	Dependent	Numeric, percentage	Measures operating profitability of a company for a financial year, taking total revenue as the basis. It is calculated as PBDITA / total revenue.
YoY growth in revenue	Dependent	Numeric, ratio	Measures growth in total revenue in comparison to prior financial year.
Major corporate restructuring	Dependent	Numeric, integer	Number of major corporate restructures (acquisition, merger, divestiture or business unit reorganization) reported during the financial year.
Dividend rate (%)	Dependent	Numeric, percentage	The rate at which the company declares dividend for the financial year as a percentage of face value of their shares.
Yield (%)	Dependent	Numeric, percentage	The rate at which the company declares dividend for the financial year as a percentage of average share price of the company's stock.
Tobin's Q	Dependent	Numeric, ratio	Approximated Tobin's Q = (MVE + PS + DEBT) / TA where MVE is the product of the firm's share price and the number of common stock shares outstanding, PS is the liquidating value of preferred stock, DEBT is the firm's short-term liabilities net of its short-term assets, plus the book value of the firm's long-term debt, and TA is the book value of total assets of the firm.

(Continued)

Table 4.1 *(Cont.)*

Variable	Type	Unit and data type	Definition / formula / explanation
MarketCap / EV	Dependent	Numeric, ratio	Ratio of average market capitalization of the company for the year and enterprise value of the firm.
Alpha	Dependent	Numeric, ratio	Excess return of the company's stock over the financial year, relative to the return of market index. This is computed as follows: If $R(i)$ = the realized return of the stock over the financial year, $R(m)$ = the realized return of the market index over the financial year, $R(f)$ = the risk-free rate of return during the financial year, β = CAPM's beta of the company's stock with respect to the market index, then, $\alpha = R(i) - [R(f) + \beta.\{R(m) - R(f)\}]$
Beta	Dependent	Numeric, ratio	Measure of volatility of the company's stock in relation to the overall market during the financial year. This is computed as (covariance of company's stock returns and market return) / variance of market return.

In order to address the variation that exists in these parameters, they are transformed to scale variables in the [0, 1] range. The converted variables used in step-wise multivariate regression are: influence of promoter directors, primacy of independent directors, presence of female directors, index of directors' presence in board meetings, index of directors' presence in other boards, index of directors' remuneration, and index of directors' presence in committees. These variables are also defined in Table 4.2.

To ensure robustness of our tests, we control for firm-specific and industry-specific factors, we use the following control variables: financial year; age of the firm in years; size of the firm; promoter's stake; non-promoters institutions' stake; industry type; and ownership type. As the value of total assets demonstrates a wide range of values across firms, we transform the values by taking natural logarithms. The control variables are defined in Table 4.3.

The statistical tests of our analysis deal with establishing causality of firm performance through corporate governance measures. We test the role of firm-level factors as well as corporate governance parameters in influencing firm performance. This is tested through step-wise multivariate regression. The regression model corresponding to these four hypotheses is depicted as:

$$y = \alpha + \beta_1 x_1 + \cdots + \beta_p x_p + \varepsilon$$

where y represents one of the 13 annual performance outcome variables; x_1 through x_p represent the firm-level independent and control variables representing

Table 4.2 Variable definitions – independent variables

Variable	Type	Unit and data type	Definition / formula / explanation
Number of directors	Independent	Numeric, integer	Number of individuals who were members of the board during the financial year.
Number of female directors	Independent	Numeric, integer	Number of female individuals who were members of the board during the financial year.
CEO duality	Independent	Binary	Indicator of whether the chairperson of the board is also the chief executive / managing director of the company during the financial year. Takes a value of 1 if chairperson = CEO / MD, 0 otherwise.
Number of executive directors	Independent	Numeric, integer	Number of company executives who were members of the board during the financial year.
Number of promoter directors	Independent	Numeric, integer	Number of individuals who were members of the board during the financial year and were original promoters or belong to promoters' families.
Number of independent directors	Independent	Numeric, integer	Number of individuals who were members of the board during the financial year and appointed by the board as independent directors.
Total no. of board meetings reported in financial year	Independent	Numeric, integer	Number of board meetings held during the financial year.
Directors' presence in board meetings	Independent	Numeric, ratio	Average number of board meetings attended by directors / total number of board meetings during the financial year.
Independent directors' presence in board meetings	Independent	Numeric, ratio	Average number of board meetings attended by independent directors / total number of board during the financial year.
Directors' presence in other boards	Independent	Numeric, ratio	Average number of other companies' boards where the directors were members for the financial year.
Directors' average remuneration (INR)	Independent	Numeric, Indian rupees (INR)	Average remuneration of all directors in a financial year, including salary, bonus and seating fees.

(Continued)

Table 4.2 (*Cont.*)

Variable	Type	Unit and data type	Definition / formula / explanation
Independent directors' average remuneration (INR)	Independent	Numeric, Indian rupees (INR)	Average remuneration of all independent directors in a financial year, including bonus and seating fees.
Directors' presence in committees	Independent	Numeric, ratio	Average number of board committees where directors were members of / total number of board committees in the financial year.
Independent directors' presence in committees	Independent	Numeric, ratio	Average number of board committees where independent directors were members of / total number of board committees in the financial year.
Influence of promoter directors	Independent	Numeric, ratio	Number of promoter directors / total number of board members during the financial year.
Primacy of independent directors	Independent	Numeric, ratio	Number of independent directors / total number of board members during the financial year.
Presence of female directors	Independent	Numeric, ratio	Number of female directors / total number of board members during the financial year.
Index of director's presence in board meetings	Independent	Numeric, ratio	Company's directors' presence in board meetings / industry average of director's presence in board meetings for the financial year.
Index of director's presence in other boards	Independent	Numeric, ratio	Company's directors' presence in others boards / industry average of director's presence in other boards for the financial year.
Index of directors' remuneration	Independent	Numeric, ratio	Company's directors' average remuneration in the company / industry average of director's remuneration for the financial year.
Index of directors' presence in committees	Independent	Numeric, ratio	Company's directors' presence in committees / industry average of director's presence in committees for the financial year.

Table 4.3 Variable definitions – control variables

Variable	Type	Unit and data type	Definition / formula / explanation
Financial year	Control	Numeric, integer	Financial year from 1998 through 2017.
Age in years	Control	Numeric, integer	Age of the firm in number of years.
Size – log (assets)	Control	Numeric, ratio	Natural logarithm of total assets at the end of the financial year.
Promoters' shares (%)	Control	Numeric, percentage	Percentage of shares held by promoters at the end of the financial year.
Non-promoter institutions' shares (%)	Control	Numeric, percentage	Percentage of shares held by non-promoter institutional shareholders at the end of the financial year.
Industry type	Control	Categorical	Possible values: non-finance companies, non-banking finance companies, banks.
Ownership type	Control	Categorical	Possible values: foreign business houses, foreign private companies, central and state government commercial enterprises, Indian business groups, Indian private companies.

age, size, concentration of ownership, and corporate governance parameters; α is the constant term; β_i is the coefficient of x_i; and ε is the error term.

In addition, as the firms come from different industry sectors, we use industry sector and financial year as the control variables for multivariate regression. We test for auto-correlation using Durbin-Watson statistics for each of the models to confirm the absence of auto-correlation.

Results and discussion

Figures 4.1, 4.2 and 4.3 provide the distribution of the sample data used for empirical analysis. The number of records are equally divided between large-cap companies and small and medium businesses. The distribution of companies by ownership shows that the majority of the records belong to companies that come from Indian business houses, however, there are sizeable number of records for government-owned companies and standalone private companies. Only a small proportion of companies belong to foreign business houses and standalone foreign businesses. Going by industry type, the majority of the records belong to non-banking, non-finance companies, from primary industries such as mining to secondary industries such as manu-facturing and tertiary segments such as services.

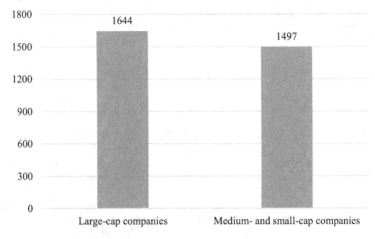

Figure 4.1 Distribution of companies by size

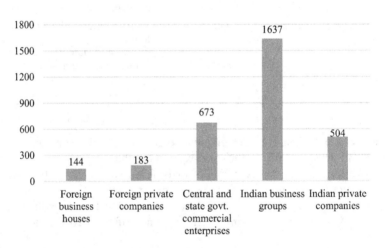

Figure 4.2 Distribution of companies by ownership

Table 4.4 provides descriptive statistics of dependent variables in the dataset used for this analysis. Return on net worth stands at an average of nearly 16 per cent, while return on assets stands at about seven per cent, and return on capital employed stands at about 11 per cent. Net profit margin stands at about seven per cent and PBDITA stands at an average of nearly 32 per cent. Average annual growth in revenue appears very high. On further investigation we noticed that several companies have reported significant changes in revenue between two consecutive years, leading to high average annual growth – but as it is not clear whether this was due to a data collection issue at the Prowess database, we do not comment any further on it.

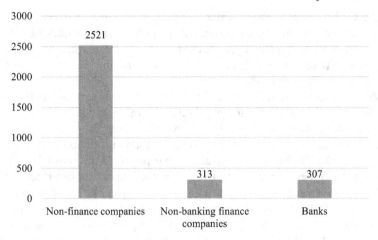

Figure 4.3 Distribution of companies by industry type

Table 4.4 Descriptive statistics of firm performance data (dependent variables)

Variable	Mean	Std. deviation
Return on net worth (%)	15.85	68.76
Return on total assets (%)	7.16	8.50
Return on capital employed (%)	11.11	37.91
Net profit margin (%)	7.03	55.92
PBDITA as % of total income (%)	31.89	33.15
YoY growth in revenue	17.47	600.58
Major corporate restructuring	1.76	1.32
Dividend rate (%)	188.97	852.32
Yield (%)	2.00	2.46
Tobin's Q	1.72	3.14
Market cap / EV	0.39	19.07
Alpha	0.27	0.43
Beta	0.99	0.39

Companies in our sample have undertaken on average just under two major corporate restructures a year. Dividend rate, on average, has been about 189 per cent with high variance, while dividend yield has been about 2 per cent. These suggest that firms in India adopt very different dividend payout policies, irrespective of their profitability, and shareholders rarely look at dividend as an important source of value when they hold stock, as the absolute value of the dividend has been significantly lower in relation to the market price of the stock. Market capitalization of stocks over enterprise value is just under 40%, suggesting that several companies have low market capitalization.

Tobin's Q, however, shows a value of 1.72, suggesting that companies, on average, do possess intangible assets. Jensen's alpha at 0.27 indicates that the companies are just a little above average in terms of market returns, and a value of nearly one for CAPM's beta indicates that the risk of the stocks are about the same as rest of the market.

Table 4.5 provides descriptive statistics of independent variables in the dataset used for this analysis. The number of directors in these companies during the period of study was just under 13, on average, while the average number of female directors has been abysmally low at less than one. In about 36 per cent of cases the CEO/MD also doubles up as the chairperson of the board. While on an average the number of executive directors in the board is about three, and the number of independent directors a little under five, the sample shows significantly lower number of promoter directors – less than one, on average – suggesting that the boards in our sample are primarily run with professionals.

The descriptive statistics also show that on an average the boards meet just over four times per year, and that on an average, each director attends 63 per cent of board meetings. This number is a little higher for independent directors at 72 per cent. The directors, on average, are extremely active in other companies' boards, sitting on more than 40 other boards! On the other hand, their presence in board committees is low – on average, out of four directors, only one would be in board committees, suggesting that a large number of board members do not participate in any committees. Directors' average

Table 4.5 Descriptive statistics of board structure, contribution and compensation (independent variables)

Variable	Mean	Std. deviation
Number of directors	12.86	5.59
Number of female directors	0.62	0.87
CEO duality	0.36	0.48
Number of executive directors	3.10	3.03
Number of promoter directors	0.78	1.57
Number of independent directors	4.62	3.06
Total no. of board meetings reported in financial year	4.09	2.17
Directors' presence in board meetings	0.63	0.13
Independent directors' presence in board meetings	0.72	0.17
Directors' presence on other boards	40.81	34.97
Directors' average remuneration (INR)	7,688,634.80	15,596,929.07
Independent directors' average remuneration (INR)	1,163,148.09	4,964,851.70
Directors' presence in committees	0.26	0.10
Independent directors' presence in committees	0.40	0.17

remuneration stands at INR 7.7 million, though we notice that variation in directors' average remuneration is very high. Independent directors' remuneration, as expected, is lower, at an average of INR 1.2 million. However, we notice high variation in independent directors' remuneration as well.

Table 4.6 provides the descriptive statistics for the control variables. The companies in the sample, on average, are mature, with an average age of more than 38 years. The average promoters' share is a little over 54 per cent, while non-promoter institutional investors hold more than 25 per cent stakes in the companies, on average.

The bivariate correlations between the variables are not found to be significant and we continue our subsequent analysis with all the variables identified for the study. We have run separate multiple regressions for each dependent variable.

Table 4.7–4.10 provide the outputs of the step-wise multiple regressions of the 13 firm performance variables. The control variables are entered in step 1 and independent variables are entered in step 2 of the regressions. Each of the categorical control variables, i.e. ownership type and industry type, are converted to (n-1) dummy variables, where n is the number of categories for the categorical variable.

The independent variables predict return on net worth statistically significantly with F $(19, 2009) = 10.676$, $p = 0.000$, Adjusted $R^2 = 0.083$. Two variables – directors' presence in board meetings and directors' remuneration – positively impact return on net worth with a p-value of 0.000, while primacy of independent directors negatively influences the outcome variable with a p-value of 0.005. The model on return on total assets is statistically significant with F $(19, 2029) = 36.563$, $p = 0.000$, Adjusted $R^2 = 0.248$. Three variables – presence of female directors, directors' presence in board meetings and directors' remuneration – positively impact return on total assets, with p-values of 0.003, 0.000 and 0.000 respectively. In addition, three other variables – CEO duality, influence of promoter directors, and primacy of independent directors – negatively influence return on total assets, with p-values of 0.000, 0.001 and 0.026 respectively. The model on return on capital employed is statistically significant with F $(19, 2024) = 2.751$, $p = 0.000$, Adjusted $R^2 = 0.016$. Only one variable – directors' remuneration – positively influences return on capital employed, with a p-value of 0.009.

Table 4.6 Descriptive statistics of control variables

Variable	Mean	Std. deviation
Financial year	-	-
Age in years	38.33	27.25
Size – log(assets)	10.78	2.49
Promoters' shares (%)	54.08	18.83
Non-promoter institutions' shares (%)	25.41	15.99
Industry type	-	-

Table 4.7 Regression results – role of corporate governance factors – Models 1, 2 and 3

Regression Summary	Model 1: Return on net worth (%)		Model 2: Return on total assets (%)		Model 3: Return on capital employed (%)	
Independent variables	Std. β	Sig	Std. β	Sig	Std. β	Sig
(Constant)		.000		.000		.187
Financial year	-.130	.000	-.133	.000	-.035	.191
Dummy_Ind1	-.030	.397	.168	.000	-.001	.986
Dummy_Ind2	.005	.863	.005	.854	-.028	.384
Dummy_FBH	.076	.003	.092	.000	.061	.019
Dummy_FP	-.057	.032	.028	.233	.030	.272
Dummy_IBG	.072	.052	.143	.000	.039	.305
Dummy_IP	.003	.915	.065	.025	.013	.695
Age	-.010	.661	-.030	.145	.001	.967
Size – log(assets)	-.168	.000	-.198	.000	-.056	.103
Promoters shares held (%)	.198	.000	.331	.000	.075	.028
Non-promoter institutions shares held (%)	.161	.000	.249	.000	.087	.010
CEO duality	-.035	.128	-.095	.000 **	-.044	.065
Influence of promoter directors	-.009	.717	-.072	.001 **	-.013	.599
Primacy of independent directors	-.069	.005 **	-.049	.026 *	.040	.110
Presence of female directors	.045	.051	.061	.003 **	.025	.291
Index of director's presence in board meetings	.087	.000 **	.077	.000 **	.011	.639
Index of director's presence in other boards	.000	.998	-.024	.254	.006	.819
Index of directors' remuneration	.116	.000 **	.212	.000 **	.064	.009 **
Index of directors' presence in committees	.008	.713	-.015	.466	.005	.837
Adjusted R^2	.083		.248		.016	
ANOVA df (d1,d2)	(19,2009)		(19,2029)		(19,2024)	
F-value and p-value	10.676; 0.000		36.563; 0.000		2.751; 0.000	

** Significant at 99%; * Significant at 95%

Table 4.8 Regression results – role of corporate governance factors – Models 4, 5 and 6

Regression Summary	Model 4: Net profit margin (%)		Model 5: PBDITA as % of total income (%)		Model 6: Growth in revenue	
Independent variables	Std. β	Sig	Std. β	Sig	Std. β	Sig
(Constant)		.000		.001		.378
Financial year	-.099	.000	-.044	.004	.024	.368
Dummy_Ind1	-.070	.036	-.735	.000	.004	.908
Dummy_Ind2	.082	.007	.053	.003	-.020	.525
Dummy_FBH	.029	.234	-.010	.511	.008	.756
Dummy_FP	.009	.710	-.037	.015	.003	.917
Dummy_IBG	.098	.007	-.013	.548	.051	.178
Dummy_IP	.030	.333	.043	.018	.005	.886
Age	-.104	.000	-.086	.000	-.039	.095
Size – log(assets)	-.015	.634	.151	.000	.003	.929
Promoters shares held (%)	.329	.000	.132	.000	-.004	.901
Non-promoter institutions shares held (%)	.257	.000	.034	.076	-.012	.720
CEO duality	.032	.149	.035	.010 *	-.012	.609
Influence of promoter directors	-.048	.035 *	-.007	.582	.003	.910
Primacy of independent directors	.002	.949	.020	.163	-.035	.164
Presence of female directors	.001	.952	.008	.561	-.029	.206
Index of director's presence in board meetings	.067	.003 **	.007	.621	-.048	.047 *
Index of director's presence in other boards	-.088	.000 **	-.039	.005 **	-.015	.542
Index of directors' remuneration	.097	.000 **	.086	.000 **	-.011	.643
Index of directors' presence in committees	-.036	.101	-.012	.380	.032	.169
Adjusted R^2	.102		.678		-.002	
ANOVA df (d1,d2)	(19,2125)		(19,2125)		(19,2121)	
F-value and p-value	13.819; 0.000		238.475; 0.000		0.809; 0.699	

** Significant at 99%; * Significant at 95%

Table 4.9 Regression results – role of corporate governance factors – Models 7, 8 and 9

Regression Summary	Model 7: Major Corp Restructuring		Model 8: Dividend Rate (%)		Model 9: Yield (%)	
Independent variables	Std. β	Sig	Std. β	Sig	Std. β	Sig
(Constant)		.000		.002		.000
Financial year	-.099	.000	.077	.003	-.206	.000
Dummy_Ind1	.013	.706	.050	.160	.162	.000
Dummy_Ind2	-.038	.219	.032	.321	.138	.000
Dummy_FBH	.093	.000	.061	.018	-.084	.010
Dummy_FP	.110	.000	.087	.001	-.143	.000
Dummy_IBG	.289	.000	.068	.070	-.265	.000
Dummy_IP	.148	.000	.028	.367	-.120	.000
Age	-.055	.015	.030	.203	-.020	.475
Size – log(assets)	.173	.000	.013	.690	.064	.103
Promoters shares held (%)	.016	.620	.147	.000	-.268	.000
Non-promoter institutions shares held (%)	.047	.144	.128	.000	-.276	.000
CEO duality	.016	.490	-.078	.001 **	-.070	.010 *
Influence of promoter directors	.029	.219	-.059	.015 *	-.065	.022 *
Primacy of independent directors	.009	.699	-.019	.443	-.053	.074
Presence of female directors	.031	.171	.030	.189	-.020	.463
Index of director's presence in board meetings	-.055	.019 *	.015	.540	-.033	.245
Index of director's presence in other boards	-.024	.306	.049	.042 *	-.025	.378
Index of directors' remuneration	-.003	.888	.180	.000 **	.022	.464
Index of directors' presence in committees	.036	.109	-.054	.020 *	.035	.204
Adjusted R^2	.057		.080		.147	
ANOVA df (d1,d2)	(19,2127)		(19,1963)		(19,1314)	
F-value and p-value	7.795; 0.000		10.101; 0.000		13.045; 0.000	

** Significant at 99%; * Significant at 95%

Table 4.10 Regression results – role of corporate governance factors – Models 10, 11, 12 and 13

Regression Summary	Model 10: Market Cap / EV		Model 11: Tobin's Q		Model 12: Alpha		Model 13: Beta	
Independent variables	Std. β	Sig	Std. β	Sig	Std. β	Sig	Std. β	Sig
(Constant)		.224		.000		.000		.000
Financial year	-.038	.257	.108	.000	-.155	.000	.273	.000
Dummy_Ind1	-.249	.000	.057	.131	-.103	.013	-.032	.427
Dummy_Ind2	-.275	.000	.036	.292	.074	.050	-.001	.972
Dummy_FBH	.005	.875	.279	.000	.082	.011	-.083	.008
Dummy_FP	.028	.375	.068	.012	.074	.013	-.002	.944
Dummy_IBG	.010	.830	.141	.000	.260	.000	-.031	.449
Dummy_IP	-.025	.451	.094	.001	.067	.035	-.050	.105
Age	.049	.093	.005	.834	-.106	.000	.070	.009
Size – log(assets)	-.026	.524	-.298	.000	-.222	.000	.152	.000
Promoters shares held (%)	.173	.000	.401	.000	.125	.002	-.218	.000
Non-promoter institutions shares held (%)	.148	.000	.254	.000	.066	.085	-.179	.000
CEO duality	.001	.965	-.109	.000 **	-.006	.819	.160	.000 **
Influence of promoter directors	-.025	.404	-.022	.381	-.038	.177	.045	.093
Primacy of independent directors	-.015	.627	-.042	.115	-.045	.128	-.060	.034 *
Presence of female directors	.042	.148	.144	.000 **	.122	.000 **	-.014	.589
Index of director's presence in board meetings	-.023	.439	.091	.000 **	.044	.120	-.142	.000 **
Index of director's presence in other boards	-.011	.699	-.030	.245	.014	.628	-.019	.481
Index of directors' remuneration	.030	.329	.201	.000 **	.002	.938	-.103	.000 **
Index of directors' presence in committees	-.020	.487	-.048	.052	.003	.905	.109	.000 **
Adjusted R^2	.066		.311		.158		.216	
ANOVA df (d1,d2)	(19,1314)		(19,1313)		(19,1312)		(19,1312)	
F-value and p-value	5.946; 0.000		32.699; 0.000		14.151; 0.000		20.250; 0.000	

** Significant at 99%; * Significant at 95%

The independent variables predict net profit margin statistically significantly with $F_{(19, 2125)} = 13.819$, $p = 0.000$, Adjusted $R^2 = 0.102$. The variables that have been found statistically significant are directors' presence in board meetings ($p = 0.003$) and directors' remuneration ($p = 0.000$), both with positive impact. In addition, the influence of promoter directors and directors' presence in other boards are found to have negative significance with p-values of 0.035 and 0.000 respectively. The model on PBDITA is statistically significant with $F_{(19, 2125)} = 238.475$, $p = 0.000$, Adjusted $R^2 = 0.678$. The variables that have been found statistically significant are CEO duality ($p = 0.010$) and directors' remuneration ($p = 0.000$), both with positive impact. In addition, directors' presence in other boards is found to have negative significance with p-value of 0.005. The model on annual revenue growth is not statistically significant, as we have $F_{(19, 2121)} = 0.809$, $p = 0.699$, Adjusted $R^2 = -0.002$.

The independent variables predict major corporate restructuring to be statistically significantly with $F_{(19, 2127)} = 7.795$, $p = 0.000$, Adjusted $R^2 = 0.057$. The variable that has been found statistically significant is directors' presence in board meetings ($p = 0.019$) with negative impact. The model on dividend is statistically significant with $F_{(19, 1963)} = 10.101$, $p = 0.000$, Adjusted $R^2 = 0.080$. The variables that have been found statistically significant are directors' presence in other boards ($p = 0.042$) and directors' remuneration ($p = 0.000$), both with positive impact. In addition, CEO duality, influence of promoter directors and directors' presence in committees are found to have negative significance with p-values of 0.001, 0.015 and 0.020 respectively in this model. The model on yield is statistically significant with $F_{(19, 1314)} = 13.045$, $p = 0.000$, Adjusted $R^2 = 0.147$. The variables that have been found statistically significant are CEO duality ($p = 0.010$) and influence of promoter directors ($p = 0.022$), both with negative impact.

The independent variables predict market-cap / EV statistically significantly with $F_{(19, 1314)} = 5.946$, $p = 0.000$, Adjusted $R^2 = 0.066$. However, no individual variable is found to be statistically significant in this model. The model on Tobin's Q is statistically significant with $F_{(19, 1313)} = 32.699$, $p = 0.000$, Adjusted $R^2 = 0.311$. The variables that have been found statistically significant are presence of female directors ($p = 0.000$), directors' presence in board meetings ($p = 0.000$), and directors' remuneration ($p = 0.000$), with positive impact. CEO duality has a negative impact on Tobin's Q with $p = 0.000$. The model on Jensen's alpha is statistically significant with $F_{(19, 1312)} = 14.151$, $p = 0.000$, Adjusted $R^2 = 0.158$. Only one independent variable – the presence of female directors – is statistically significant with positive impact ($p = 0.000$). The model on CAPM's beta is statistically significant with $F_{(19, 1312)} = 20.250$, $p = 0.000$, Adjusted $R^2 = 0.216$. Two independent variables, CEO duality ($p = 0.000$) and directors' presence in committees ($p = 0.000$) are found to be statistically significant with positive impact. In addition, primacy of independent directors, directors' presence in board meetings, and directors' remuneration are found to have statistically significant negative impact on CAPM's beta, with p-values of 0.034, 0.000 and 0.000 respectively.

As the results show in Tables 4.7–4.10, the absence of CEO duality in SOEs positively influences return on total assets, dividend rate, yield, and Tobin's Q, though it appears to have a negative influence on PBDITA and CAPM's beta, i.e. if CEO duality is present, firms tend to have higher market risks. The influence of promoters on the board has a negative impact on return on total assets, net profit margin, dividend rate, and yield. Primacy of independent directors on the board negatively influences return on net worth, return on total assets, as well as CAPM's beta. Presence of female directors positively influences return on total assets, Tobin's Q, as well as Jensen's alpha. Directors' presence in board meetings positively affects return on net worth, return on total assets, net profit margin and Tobin's Q, while it has a negative effect on the number of corporate restructures. Directors' presence in other boards positively affects dividend rate, and it negatively affects net profit margin, and PBDITA. Directors' remuneration positively affects return on net worth, return on total assets, return on capital employed, net profit margin, PBDITA, dividend rate, Tobin's Q, and it negatively affects CAPM's beta, i.e. higher remuneration leads to reduced market risks. Directors' presence in committees positively influences CAPM's beta, and negatively influences dividend rate. The following section discusses the influence of these significant variables in detail.

Composition of the board and diversity of board members

Adams and Ferreira (2009), in a study on top European firms, find that women tend to have better attendance records at board meetings than their male counterparts. Specifically, they note that the likelihood that: a female director has attendance problems is lower than that of a male director; male directors have fewer attendance problems when there is a greater proportion of female directors on the board; firms with more diverse boards provide their directors with more pay-performance incentives; and firms with more diverse boards have more board meetings.

Studies have also found that women are more likely to sit on audit, governance and nominating committees. Gender-diverse boards allocate more time and effort to monitoring, and diverse boards are more likely to hold CEOs accountable for poor stock-driven performance. Such an atmosphere of accountability would undoubtedly change the way the board makes decisions (Leblanc & Gillies, 2010).

Our findings on Indian firms are in line with these observations. Three of our firm performance variables – return on total assets, Tobin's Q, and Jensen's alpha – are significantly and positively influenced by the presence of female directors. Tobin's Q is a representation of the market's assessment of the firm, including its future prospects, and provides a measure of the management's ability to generate future income stream from an asset base (Short & Keasey, 1999). Therefore, a diverse board may demonstrate actions that the market desires and appreciates, and therefore has a positive influence on the market's view of the firm's worth.

Conversely, the presence of promoter directors on the board negatively impacts return on total assets, net profit margin, dividend payout, and dividend yield, suggesting that the promoter directors may not be able to contribute to the value creation of firms, and may look at board positions more as an entitlement than as a responsibility.

We also notice that the primacy of independent directors negatively influences return on net worth, return on total assets, and CAPM's beta. This leads us to the conjecture that independent directors, despite high expectations, have not been able to drive the performance of organizations. This rings a bell with what we have observed in the Satyam case, where an illustrious board of independent directors were not able to make the right decision for the company. Such ineffectiveness can be attributed to three factors: (a) the independent directors suffer from information asymmetry, i.e. they are presented limited information by the executive, and at times key information may not be shared with them; (b) the independent directors do not take an active interest in the happenings of the company, due to their primary preoccupations and other responsibilities; or (c) the independent directors, having been chosen by the chairperson / CEO to serve the boards, choose to remain loyal to the chairperson / CEO.

Contribution and involvement of board members

Attending board meetings regularly is considered a hallmark of the conscientious director. Only a board member who attends and participates in board meetings regularly may be in a position to assess issues and take effective decisions. There is a widespread perception that high-profile board members rarely show up for meetings, and when they do show up, they are not prepared (Sonnenfeld, 2002). Research also indicates that the frequency of board meetings attended by directors has a positive and significant effect on a firm's profitability.

Our findings are in line with these observations. We find that return on net worth, return on total assets, net profit margin and Tobin's Q are positively and significantly influenced by directors' attendance at board meetings. As explained before, Tobin's Q is a representation of the market's assessment of the firm, and if the market notices active participation by board members in board meetings, it influences the market's view of the firm's worth positively. Directors' participation in board meetings also has a negative influence on CAPM's beta, suggesting reduced volatility in stock market performance. In addition, we notice that directors' participation in board meetings also leads to fewer corporate restructuring activities.

We find conflicting results on directors' participation in other boards. Based on past research, we have argued that if board members were also members in other companies' boards then they would get a higher level of exposure on governance issues, challenges and solutions. This would not only broaden their world-view of governance, but would also enable them to make better decisions and guide the company's management better. However, we find that directors' participation positively influences equity dividend and negatively influences net profit margin and PBDITA. Further research is required to understand the moderating role of directors' participation in other boards on firm performance.

We also find unexpected results on directors' participation in board-level committees. The statistical analysis shows that higher participation in board-level committees tends to have a negative impact on dividend payout and a positive influence on CAPM's beta. Thus, the sample data suggest that directors' participation in board-level committees has no impact on most of the firm performance measures and has limited negative impact on returns to shareholders and volatility of stock prices in the market. Further research is required to understand how directors' participation in board meetings contributes to firm performance.

Our test on CEO duality suggests that companies where the CEO / MD also doubles up as the chairperson tend to be negatively influenced on several performance variables, such as return on assets, dividend rate, yield and Tobin's Q. In addition, CEO duality also tends to increase CAPM's beta, suggesting higher volatility in the stock market. Thus, as the CEO plays the role of agent as well as that of principal, we see evidence of the agency effect, where the CEO / MD weakens the power of the rest of the directors, and in the process may end up making value-destroying decisions for the company. This finds support in the argument of White and Ingrassia (1992). However, in this sample we also notice that CEO duality has a weak positive influence on PBDITA.

Compensation to board members

We find strong statistical support for our argument that directors' remuneration positively impacts on the functioning of the board, resulting in superior firm performance. Our empirical tests find that directors' remuneration has a positive impact on return on net worth, return on total assets, return on capital employed, net profit margin, PBDITA, dividend payout, and Tobin's Q. In addition, directors' remuneration has a negative impact on CAPM's beta, suggesting that a highly compensated board may drive down volatility of share prices in the market.

In summary, our key findings show that if the board is diverse, board attendance is maintained well, CEO duality is absent, and the board is compensated well, then the board brings in a positive outlook and superior decision-making for the company, and that in turn raises the value of the firm, not just in accounting measures, but also in market measures and returns to the shareholders.

Lessons from the Satyam saga

Satyam Computers, at the time of the debacle, had independent directors who were professionally competent to play their expected roles in the board. So, one would wonder, why didn't they deliver? Did they play along with the CEO because the CEO had invited them to join the board?

An individual independent director may not play an effective role in the board in isolation. Even if a particular independent director is highly committed, she can at best initiate a discussion, but cannot stop a decision by herself even if it is detrimental to the interest of shareholders or other stakeholders. Nor can she blow the whistle outside the boardroom (e.g. to regulators) because board proceedings are considered confidential. However, as a group they can act collectively to stop inappropriate resolutions proposed by the CEO or other directors. However, turning independent directors into policemen in the boardroom may be detrimental to the independence of directors, the freedom of enterprise of the managers and the costs of governance.

Thus, to ensure adequate and effective internal controls the board must depend on other institutional apparatus of corporate governance, such as internal audit, external audit, and legal counsel. Specifically, the audit committee of the board should be able to identify signals that indicate potential concerns and value-destroying initiatives.

Investigation into the Satyam case revealed that the accounting fraud had been perpetrated over a long period of five to seven years. Moreover, as reported in many newspapers, some Satyam clients, including the World Bank, had been complaining of fraudulent and unethical practices by the company before the scandal broke out in 2009. In addition, when it was proposed that the company expand into the completely unrelated business of infrastructure and construction, floated by the chairman's family members, the independent directors did not apparently object to that. This leads to the conjecture that the independent directors lacked commitment, at least collectively.

This brings us to the fundamental question of what incentives for directors are effective to ensure their commitment to board responsibilities. At a theoretical level, two types of incentives work: (a) a monetary incentive, which is to compensate independent directors adequately; and (b) the threat of losing hard-earned social stature and personal reputation. It appears that both types of incentive failed in case of Satyam.

According to newspaper reports, in the year preceding the fraud each individual director of Satyam received around INR 1.3 million to carry out their board responsibilities. Considering that an independent director on average devotes about 100 hours per annum to carry out board responsibilities, this sum of compensation would appear attractive, even by western standards. Incidentally, Prof Palepu had received INR 8.7 million from the company in the prior year towards consultancy fees for his services. It should be noted that Prof Palepu was also a director at Global Trust Bank that collapsed due to an accounting scam in 2002.

Behavioural scientists suggest that if an individual considers certain responsibilities as peripheral, and if the chance of failure in performing those duties coming to light is low, it is likely that he will shirk those responsibilities, as the cost of failure to the individual is low. Independent directors, being rational human beings, seemed to behave in a similar manner in the Satyam case. In addition, if regulators are lax in regularly assessing the performance of the board, directly or indirectly through scrutiny of filings, and if law enforcement agencies are not swift in penalizing erring independent directors, the corporate governance framework, however robust in definition, remains ineffective.

The Satyam scandal was a watershed moment for corporate governance practices in India, and several agencies initiated corrective measures to avoid similar situations in the future. After the scandal, the Confederation of Indian Industries (CII) set up a task force to suggest reforms. The National Association of Software and Services Companies (NASSCOM) established a corporate governance and ethics committee which suggested reforms relating to audit committees, shareholder rights, and whistle-blower policy. SEBI's committee on disclosure and accounting standards issued a discussion paper in 2009 to deliberate on voluntary adoption of international financial reporting standards (IFRS), appointment of chief financial officers by audit committees based on qualifications, experience, and background, and rotation of auditors every five years to avoid familiarity leading to corporate malpractice and mismanagement. Subsequently, in 2010, SEBI amended the Listing Agreement to include a provision dealing with the appointment of a chief financial officer.

In 2009, the Ministry of Corporate Affairs of India issued a set of voluntary guidelines for corporate governance in the areas of independence of independent directors, roles and responsibilities of audit committees, whistle-blower policies, separation of the offices of the chairman and the CEO to ensure independence, terms and conditions of the appointment of directors – such as their tenures, remuneration, evaluation, and the issuance of a formal letter of appointment – and placing limits on the number of companies in which an individual could be a director. Subsequently, in 2013, the Companies Act 1956 was amended, and it incorporated several provisions to strengthen corporate governance practices in India. These are discussed in Chapter 5.

Thus corporate governance after the Satyam scandal has to be in conformity with the amended Companies Act and other guidelines. This scandal also exposed the role of dishonest external auditors and has forced the government to provide for checks and balances.

Conclusions

In this chapter we have carried out detailed empirical analysis on how corporate governance parameters, especially board composition, contribution of the board members and compensation of the board members, contribute to firm performance. We have analysed the case of Satyam Computers, where serious fraud had been perpetrated by the CEO and the executive team for years, with a highly qualified set of independent directors remaining completely clueless about the situation, until the CEO admitted to the fraud. This eventually led to a near-complete wipe-out of shareholders' wealth.

Having noticed such events, some would argue for directors to become vigilant about companies' day-to-day operations; however, that may lead to a breed of "super-managers", with lack of trust in managerial decision-making. What is probably acceptable is paying attention to structuring a balanced board and ensuring the board contributes effectively. Towards this we have evaluated the role of corporate governance parameters involving board composition, contribution and involvement of board members, and compensation of board members. We have tested how these influence a series of firm performance factors, comprising accounting performance, growth factors, and market performance, including shareholder returns.

The empirical analysis of data from 200 Indian companies over a period of 20 years broadly suggests that diversity of the board, measured through the presence of female directors, and limited influence of promoter directors do contribute to positive performance. The presence of female board members brings in balance to the board composition and conveys the message of good corporate governance and a firm's ethical behaviour. We find that a higher presence of independent directors does not benefit the firms, suggesting that independent directors may need to move beyond the "ceremonial position" and contribute to value-creation for the firm through involvement and superior decision-making. In terms of contribution and involvement of the board members, we observe that directors' participation in board meetings has a positive effect on several performance parameters. We do not see any benefit of directors' presence in committees on firm performance; however, considering that average participation in board-level committees is very low, we argue that higher involvement of directors in board-level committees is required for any meaningful conclusion to be drawn on this factor. In addition, directors' participation in other companies' boards does not provide us any conclusive results and we need further studies on this factor. We also find that CEO duality, i.e. the CEO / MD performing the role of chairperson of the board, has a negative impact on several performance measures, suggesting the presence of agency effect and weakening of the power of the other directors in such situations. We find strong support for directors' remuneration positively influencing several firm performance measures, suggesting that superior remuneration may lead to a higher sense of responsibility and ownership in the directors, which leads to superior, value-creating decisions in the board.

The Satyam scandal not only brought an improved awareness level among the shareholders, regulatory agencies, auditors and other multilateral bodies responsible for corporate governance, but it also led to the enactment of new regulatory frameworks. The most important of these was the Companies' Act 2013 (CA2013). The introduction of CA2013 in India had specific objectives from a corporate governance perspective. These were around responsibility of independent directors, board size, presence of female directors and participation in board meetings. Chapter 5 discusses how CA2013 attempted to bring in changes in corporate governance practices in the country.

References and further reading

Adams, R. B., & Ferreira, D. (2009). Women in the boardroom and their impact on governance and performance. *Journal of Financial Economics*, 94(2), 291–309.

Anderson, C. A., & Anthony, R. N. (1986). *The New Corporate Directors: Insights for Board Members and Executives*. Hoboken, NJ: Wiley.

Balasubramanian, N. (2010). *Corporate Governance and Stewardship: Emerging Role and Responsibilities of Corporate Boards and Directors*. New York: McGraw Hill Education.

Cadbury, S. A. (2000). The corporate governance agenda. *Corporate Governance: An International Review*, 8(1), 7–15.

Carter, D. A., Simkins, B. J., & Simpson, W. G. (2003). Corporate governance, board diversity, and firm value. *Financial Review*, 38(1), 33–53.

Chiang, H. T., & Chia, F. (2005). An empirical study of corporate governance and corporate performance. *Journal of American Academy of Business*, 6(1), 95–101.

Chakrabarti, R., Megginson, W., & Yadav, P. K. (2008). Corporate governance in India. *Journal of Applied Corporate Finance*, 20(1), 59–72.

Charan, R. (2011). *Boards that Deliver: Advancing Corporate Governance from Compliance to Competitive Advantage (Vol. 20)*. Hoboken, NJ: John Wiley & Sons.

Conger, J. A., Finegold, D., & Lawler, E. E. (1998). Appraising boardroom performance. *Harvard Business Review*, 76(1), 136–164.

Daily, C. M., Dalton, D. R., & Cannella, A. A. (2003). Corporate governance: Decades of dialogue and data. *Academy of Management Review*, 28(3), 371–382.

Dalton, D. R., Daily, C. M., Ellstrand, A. E., & Johnson, J. L. (1998). Number of directors and financial performance: A meta-analysis. *Academy of Management Journal*, 42(6), 674–686.

Desai (2014). *Companies Act Series*. Nishith Desai Associates. Available at: www.nish ithdesai.com/information/research-and-articles/nda-hotline/companies-act-series.htm l. Last accessed 23 September 2015.

Donaldson, L. (1990). The ethereal hand: Organizational economics and management theory. *Academy of Management Review*, 15(3), 369–381.

Donaldson, L., & Davis, J. H. (1991). Stewardship theory or agency theory: CEO governance and shareholder returns. *Australian Journal of Management*, 16(1), 49–64.

Dwivedi, N., & Jain, A. K. (2005). Corporate governance and performance of Indian firms: The effect of board size and ownership. *Employee Responsibilities and Rights Journal*, 17(3), 161–172.

Fama, E. F. (1980). Agency problems and the theory of the firm. *Journal of Political Economy*, 88(2), 288–307.

Fama, E. F., & Jensen, M. C. (1983). Separation of ownership and control. *Journal of Law and Economics*, 26(2), 301–325.

Ferris, S. P., Jagannathan, M., & Pritchard, A. C. (2003). Too busy to mind the business? Monitoring by directors with multiple board appointments. *Journal of Finance*, 58(3), 1087–1111.

Goilden, B. R., & Zajac, E. J. (2001). When will boards influence strategy? Inclination × power = strategic change. *Strategic Management Journal*, 22(2), 1087–1117.

Gregory, H. J. (2000). *International Comparison of Corporate Governance Guidelines and Codes of Best Practice*. New York: Weil. Gotshal & Manges LLP.

Harris, I. C., & Shimizu, K. (2004). Too busy to serve? An examination of the influence of overboarded directors. *Journal of Management Studies*, 41(5), 775–798.

IICA (2015). *Corporate Governance*. New Delhi: Indian Institute of Corporate Affairs, Taxmann Publications.

Jensen, M. C. (1993). The modern industrial revolution, exit, and the failure of internal control systems. *Journal of Finance*, 48(3), 831–880.

Jensen, M. C. (2001). Value maximization, stakeholder theory, and the corporate objective function. *Journal of Applied Corporate Finance*, 14(3), 8–21.

John, K., & Senbet, L. W. (1998). Corporate governance and board effectiveness. *Journal of Banking and Finance*, 22(4), 371–403.

KPMG (2014). *Companies Act 2013: Raising the Bar on Governance*. KPMG. Available at: www.kpmg.com/IN/en/Documents/Companies_Act_2013_Raising_the_bar_on_Governance.pdf. Last accessed 23 September 2015.

Leblanc, R., & Gillies, J. (2010). *Inside the Boardroom: How Boards Really Work and the Coming Revolution in Corporate Governance*. Hoboken, NJ: John Wiley & Sons.

Lipton, M., & Lorsch, J. W. (1992). A modest proposal for improved corporate governance. *The Business Lawyer*, 48, 59–77.

Miwa, Y., & Ramseyer, J. M. (2000). Corporate governance in transitional economies: Lessons from the prewar Japanese cotton textile industry. *The Journal of Legal Studies*, 29(1), 171–203.

Murphy, K. J. (1999). Executive compensation. In O. Ashenfelter and D. Card (eds.) *Handbook of Labor Economics (Vol. 3, Part B)*, 2485–2563. Amsterdam: Elsevier.

OECD (1999). *OECD Principles of Corporate Governance*. Paris: OECD.

Pearce, J. A., & Zahra, S. A. (1992). Board composition from a strategic contingency perspective. *Journal of Management Studies*, 29(4), 411–438.

Prasad, R. S. (2014). Corporate governance in India: Challenges for emerging economic super power. *Business Studies Journal*, 6(2), 1–17.

Short, H., & Keasey, K. (1999). Managerial ownership and the performance of firms: Evidence from the UK. *Journal of Corporate Finance*, 5(1), 79–101.

Smith, N., Smith, V., & Verner, M. (2006). Do women in top management affect firm performance? A panel study of 2,500 Danish firms. *International Journal of Productivity and Performance Management*, 55(7), 569–593.

Sonnenfeld, J. A. (2002). What makes great boards great. *Harvard Business Review*, 80(9), 106–113.

Tricker, R. B., & Tricker, R. I. (2015). *Corporate Governance: Principles, Policies, and Practices* (3rd edn). Oxford: Oxford University Press.

White, J. B., & Ingrassia, P. (1992). Eminence grise: Behind revolt at GM, lawyer Ira Millstein helped call the shots. *Wall Street Journal*, April 13.

Yermack, D. (1996). Higher market valuation of companies with a small board of directors. *Journal of Financial Economics*, 40(2), 185–211.

Zhu, Y., Tian, G. G., & Ma, S. (2009). Executive compensation, board characteristics and firm performance in China: The impact of compensation committee. 22nd Australasian Finance and Banking Conference, Sydney, 16–18 December.

5 Board characteristics

Long-term trends and impact of Companies Act 2013

Introduction of Companies Act 2013

With the introduction of the Companies Act 2013 (CA2013), we expect significant improvement in corporate governance practices in India. This section studies some of the key corporate governance practices of large Indian corporations post CA2013 implementation and evaluates their moderating role on firm performance.

As mentioned in Chapter 3, the introduction of CA2013 by the Indian government has witnessed several key changes with respect to the earlier 1956 Companies Act in areas concerned with the management and governance of companies. These changes are aimed at ensuring higher standards of transparency and accountability, and seek to align the corporate governance practices in India with global best practices, raising the bar on governance (Desai, 2014; KPMG, 2014). The important aspects of CA2013 that help companies assess the impact and develop a strategy around compliance and corporate governance are: (a) responsibility of independent directors; (b) a maximum limit of 15 on number of directors; (c) presence of at least one female director; and (d) flexibility of participation in board meetings through audio- or video-conferences. In addition, CA2013 specifies that there must be at least four committees where board members should participate: an audit committee, a nomination and remuneration committee, a corporate social responsibility committee and a stakeholder's relationship committee (KPMG, 2014).

Specifically, CA2013 clearly defined the responsibility and accountability of independent directors and auditors. In addition, it calls for restrictions on auditors performing certain non-audit services such as consulting and advisory services. CA2013 mandates compulsory rotation of auditors and audit firms, including a cooling-off period following one term as an auditor. An auditor would not be able to perform non-audit services for the company and its holding and subsidiary companies. It also specifies that the auditors are expected to report fraudulent acts if they notice them while performing their duties (MCA, 2013).

As per CA2013, independent directors have been barred from receiving stock options and are not entitled to receive remuneration for their services, except for reimbursements and sitting fees. This is to ensure that they are not influenced to compromise their independence for pecuniary gains. The act also specifies larger roles for independent directors in the audit committee and the remuneration committee. CA2013 also insists on at least one female director on a company's board.

Another critical reform brought in by CA2013 concerned performance management and the reporting of the directors on the board. Companies are now expected to disclose the details of formal evaluation and performance of their directors. In terms of protection of shareholder interests, CA2013 provides for initiating class action suits against the company and its auditors for damages.

Long-term trend analysis of board characteristics

Based on the empirical data collected from CMIE Prowess and NSE Infobase, long-term trends of board characteristics have been plotted to understand the changes that have taken place in Indian boards. Figure 5.1 shows the trend in average number of directors on the boards in our sample of 200 companies. We also separately plot data for large-cap companies and small- and medium-cap companies. We notice that the number of board members has gone up a little since 1999 from about 10 to about 15, a number recommended in CA2013. It is also noticed that large-cap companies tend to have a larger board.

Figure 5.2 shows that the average number of female directors was abysmally low in 1999 at 0.2, i.e. in five boards together, there was just one female director. And this number was even lower for medium- and small-cap companies. The average has improved over time, especially after the introduction of CA2013, and the trend is similar for both groups of companies.

As depicted in Figure 5.3, CEO duality – i.e. CEO / MD also doubling up as chairman of the board – was present in about 35 per cent boards in 1999;

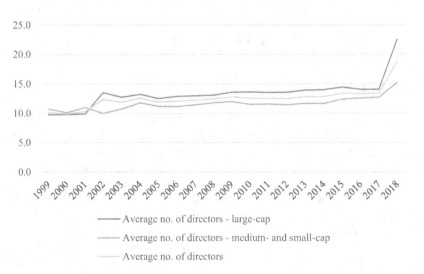

Figure 5.1 Trend in number of directors

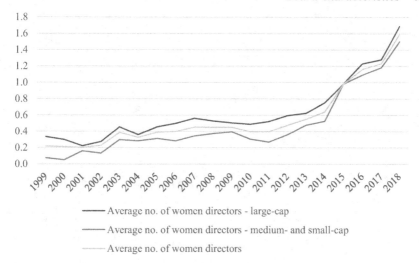

Figure 5.2 Trend in number of female directors

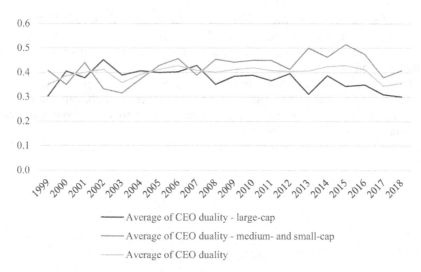

Figure 5.3 Trend in CEO duality

the number has not changed much over time. However, we notice that in the past decade, CEO duality has remained more prevalent in medium- and small-cap companies, in comparison to large-cap companies.

Figure 5.4 shows the trend in average number of executive directors in Indian companies has grown from an average of less than one to more than four by the end of 2018. Large-cap companies maintained a higher proportion of executive directors.

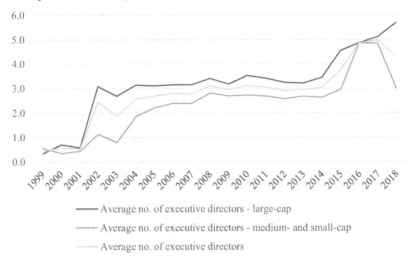

Figure 5.4 Trend in number of executive directors

Trend in number of promoter directors on the board is depicted in Figure 5.5. The average number has gone up over 20 years and promoter directors are present in higher numbers in medium- and small-cap companies than they are in large-cap companies.

Figure 5.6 shows the trend in average number of independent directors, which has seen a significant rise over the past 20 years. Large-cap companies maintained a higher number of independent directors in comparison to medium- and small-cap companies.

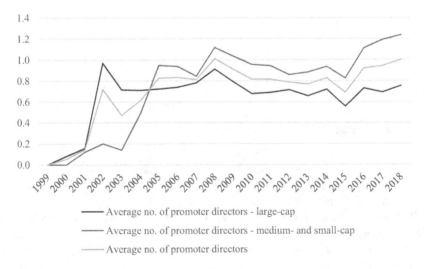

Figure 5.5 Trend in number of promoter directors

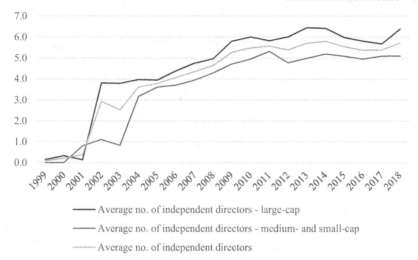

Figure 5.6 Trend in number of independent directors

We also plot primacy of independent directors on the board. Primacy is computed as the ratio of independent directors to total number of directors in the board. The past decade has witnessed a primacy value of 0.3 and above, suggesting that at least 30 per cent or more of the directors on the board have been independent directors. In addition, we note that the measure has converged for large-cap and medium- and small-cap companies.

Figure 5.8 plots directors' presence in board meetings; it appears the number has remained flat, both for large-cap and medium- and small-cap companies.

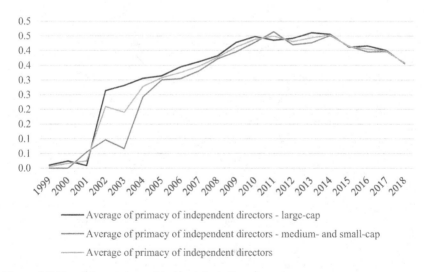

Figure 5.7 Trend in primacy of independent directors

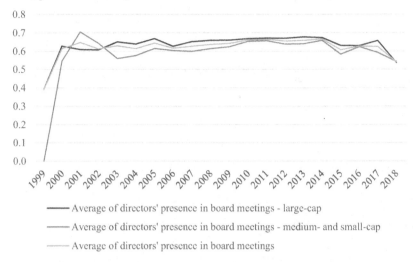

Figure 5.8 Trend in directors' presence in board meetings

Similarly, as Figure 5.9 shows, independent directors' presence in board meetings has shown marginal increase over the past decade; the trend is applicable for both groups of companies.

In Figure 5.10 we plot directors' presence in other companies' boards. It is surprising to see that, on average, a large number of directors are present in other companies' boards, especially the directors of large-cap companies.

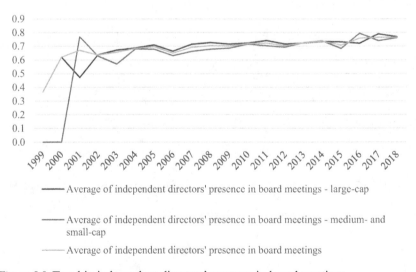

Figure 5.9 Trend in independent directors' presence in board meetings

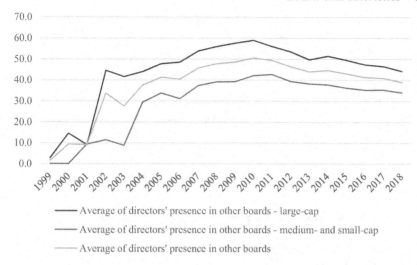

Figure 5.10 Trend in directors' presence in other boards

Directors' average remuneration, as shown in Figure 5.11, has had a sharp growth trajectory in the past decade. In particular, directors' remuneration in large-cap companies has grown significantly, creating a wider gap in directors' average remuneration between the two groups of companies.

Similarly, as shown in Figure 5.12, independent directors' remuneration has gone up significantly after the introduction of CA2013. Here again, the rise is much steeper for directors in large-cap companies.

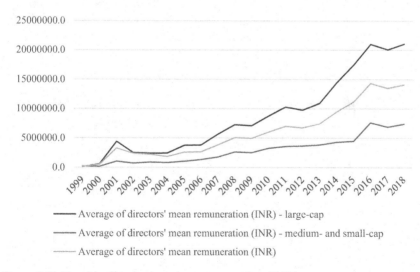

Figure 5.11 Trend in directors' average remuneration (INR)

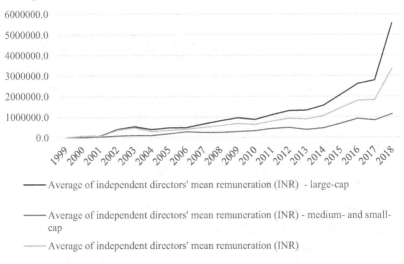

Figure 5.12 Trend in independent directors' average remuneration

Figure 5.13 depicts directors' presence in board committees. The past decade has witnessed the average presence of directors in board committees of both large-cap and medium- and small-cap companies converge to about 0.3 – i.e. on an average a director is present in about 0.3 committees. Fiscal 2018 also witnessed a reduction in directors' presence in committees.

On similar lines, as Figure 5.14 shows, independent directors' presence has remained static over the past decade, and there is not much of a difference between large-cap and medium- and small-cap companies.

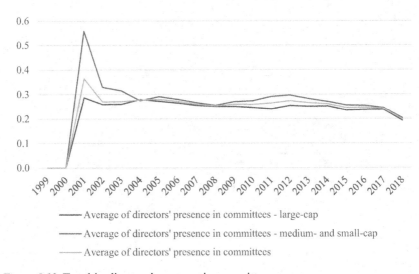

Figure 5.13 Trend in directors' presence in committees

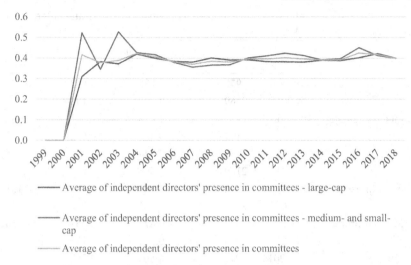

———— Average of independent directors' presence in committees - large-cap

———— Average of independent directors' presence in committees - medium- and small-cap

———— Average of independent directors' presence in committees

Figure 5.14 Trend in independent directors' presence in committees

Effect of CA2013 on board composition and contribution of the board

In this section we conduct a comparative analysis of board characteristics between pre-CA2013 and post CA2013. As the initial CA2013 rollout included binding regulations and recommendations, it is expected that some organizations would adopt CA2013 clauses for improvement in corporate governance in letter and spirit, while other organizations would take time to change.

Table 5.1 provides the segregated group statistics of board characteristics for the years before fiscal 2014 and the years 2014 and after.

We conducted independent sample t-tests (see Table 5.2) to evaluate if the differences between these two groups (before fiscal 2014 and afterwards) are statistically significant. We find that there is a significant difference in the number of directors on the board – after the introduction of CA2013 the average number of directors in our sample went up significantly.

In addition, we observe that the number of female directors has also increased significantly. However, there is no change in CEO duality, though CA2013 recommends that the CEO / MD should not double up as the chairperson of the board. The number of executive directors has increased significantly, the number of promoter directors has gone up marginally, and number of independent directors has also gone up significantly. This suggests that the expansion of the board size, post CA2013, has primarily been effected by inclusion of female directors, executive directors and independent directors.

The number of board meetings has gone up significantly, and so has directors' presence in board meetings. However, we also notice that independent directors' presence in board meetings has gone down significantly during this time, suggesting that while the overall involvement of board members has on

Table 5.1 Descriptive statistics – governance parameters before and after implementation of CA2013

Variable	Financial year	N	Mean	Std. deviation	Std. error mean
Number of directors	>= 2014	972	14.330	7.662	0.246
	< 2014	2169	12.207	4.198	0.090
Number of female directors	>= 2014	972	1.123	1.013	0.033
	< 2014	2169	0.401	0.692	0.015
CEO duality	>= 2014	972	0.344	0.475	0.015
	< 2014	2169	0.366	0.482	0.010
Number of executive directors	>= 2014	972	4.201	4.093	0.131
	< 2014	2169	2.612	2.246	0.048
Number of promoter directors	>= 2014	972	0.876	1.557	0.050
	< 2014	2169	0.731	1.579	0.034
Number of independent directors	>= 2014	972	5.564	2.263	0.073
	< 2014	2169	4.201	3.275	0.070
Total no. of board meetings reported	>= 2014	972	4.612	1.616	0.052
	< 2014	2169	3.861	2.340	0.050
Directors' presence in board meetings	>= 2014	947	0.613	0.139	0.005
	< 2014	1724	0.642	0.124	0.003
Independent directors' presence in board meetings	>= 2014	929	0.746	0.171	0.006
	< 2014	1526	0.698	0.174	0.004
Directors' presence in other boards	>= 2014	972	41.712	29.061	0.932
	< 2014	2169	40.402	37.318	0.801
Directors' average remuneration	>= 2014	946	12562016.752	21500293.414	699034.835
	< 2014	1641	4879238.496	9778764.512	241395.793
Independent directors' average remuneration	>= 2014	891	1925851.584	7629234.293	255588.966
	< 2014	1303	641606.405	1030089.504	28536.635
Directors' presence in committees	>= 2014	864	0.238	0.093	0.003
	< 2014	1543	0.266	0.105	0.003
Independent directors' presence in committees	>= 2014	859	0.405	0.178	0.006
	< 2014	1403	0.392	0.169	0.005

average increased post CA2013, there are still a large number of independent directors across companies who do not regularly participate in board meetings, which weakens the board-level decision-making process. Interestingly, directors' presence in other boards has gone up. The question one might ask is why do the directors join boards when they will not participate in board meetings?

Table 5.2 t-Test – Difference in governance parameters before and after implementation of CA2013

Variable		Levene's test for equality of variances		t-test for equality of means		
		F	Sig.	t	df	Sig. (2-tailed)
Number of directors	Equal variances assumed	7.355	.007	9.986	3139.000	0.000
	Equal variances not assumed			8.109	1239.698	0.000 **
Number of female directors	Equal variances assumed	80.247	.000	23.247	3139.000	0.000
	Equal variances not assumed			20.213	1391.506	0.000 **
CEO duality	Equal variances assumed	6.217	.013	-1.212	3139.000	0.226
	Equal variances not assumed			-1.219	1892.145	0.223
Number of executive directors	Equal variances assumed	5.301	.021	13.980	3139.000	0.000
	Equal variances not assumed			11.357	1240.543	0.000 **
Number of promoter directors	Equal variances assumed	4.216	.040	2.386	3139.000	0.017
	Equal variances not assumed			2.398	1892.182	0.017 *
Number of independent directors	Equal variances assumed	221.725	.000	11.770	3139.000	0.000
	Equal variances not assumed			13.480	2616.573	0.000 **
Total no. of board meetings reported	Equal variances assumed	139.602	.000	9.087	3139.000	0.000
	Equal variances not assumed			10.409	2618.334	0.000 **
Directors' presence in board meetings	Equal variances assumed	7.055	.008	-5.590	2669.000	0.000
	Equal variances not assumed			-5.410	1769.906	0.000**
Independent directors' presence in board meetings	Equal variances assumed	.370	.543	6.693	2453.000	0.000 **
	Equal variances not assumed			6.721	1986.506	0.000

Table 5.2 (*Cont.*)

Variable		Levene's test for equality of variances		t-test for equality of means		
		F	Sig.	t	df	Sig. (2-tailed)
Directors' presence in other boards	Equal variances assumed	53.741	.000	0.970	3139.000	0.332
	Equal variances not assumed			1.065	2359.299	0.287
Directors' average remuneration	Equal variances assumed	139.654	.000	12.419	2585.000	0.000
	Equal variances not assumed			10.389	1174.201	0.000 **
Independent directors' average remuneration	Equal variances assumed	35.538	.000	5.997	2192.000	0.000
	Equal variances not assumed			4.994	912.231	0.000 **
Directors' presence in committees	Equal variances assumed	8.565	.003	-6.624	2405.000	0.000
	Equal variances not assumed			-6.860	1977.590	0.000 **
Independent directors' presence in committees	Equal variances assumed	2.203	.138	1.781	2260.000	0.075
	Equal variances not assumed			1.757	1736.493	0.079

** Significant at 99%; * Significant at 95%

Directors' total average remuneration has gone up significantly over time, and so has independent directors' total remuneration. Though CA2013 insists on no incentives or compensation to independent directors, and that they should be paid only reimbursements and sitting fees, the data shows that the clause may not have been implemented in totality.

Directors' participation in board-level committees, especially executive directors' participation, has come down significantly. Again, the question is why would directors be paid handsomely when they do not get involved in board-level committees which investigate most of the critical issues before decisions are made?

Impact of board characteristics changes on firm performance

Our previous analysis indicates that since the introduction of CA2013 board composition has changed significantly, boards' contribution to corporate governance activities have also changed, and so has the compensation of the board members. In this section we study how these changes make a difference in firm performance. We conducted a step-wise multivariate regression analysis, similar to in Chapter 4, with an additional control variable factoring in the CA2013 introduction. In the interests of brevity the full regression results are not presented here, however, the results are similar to those of Chapter 4, i.e. we observe a similar influence of corporate governance parameters on firm performance. We also notice that the higher presence of female directors post introduction of CA2013 has additional positive influence on some of the performance variables.

Have Indian boards transitioned from their ceremonial nature?

Past data and cases, including the case of Satyam Computer Services discussed in the previous chapter, show that Indian boards used to be primarily ceremonial in nature, as was the case in most parts of the world during the 20th century. A ceremonial board consists of directors who serve the board for prestige and perks, have little knowledge about the company, and concur with the CEO's decision in all board deliberations (Charan, 2011). In the US, post Enron scandal and implementation of SOX, most boards moved from their ceremonial status to "liberated" status, as the directors started asking questions – questions about the company's performance, questions about business risks, and questions about managerial decisions. The regulatory changes and demands from investors forced the directors to take their fiduciary responsibilities seriously. However, the results in our analysis do not conclusively suggest that Indian boards, on average, have moved away from ceremonial status – while composition of the board has improved, contribution and involvement of board members have not changed much in the past 20 years.

A liberated board is expected to undergo further transformation to a "progressive" board, where the board members become effective not just as competent individuals, but as a collective team as well. Charan (2011) posits that in such a board the directors form coherent groups, and contribute to the dialogue in board meetings and committee meetings. They may challenge each other, but they do that through intellectual exchanges, remaining objective, and without breaking the harmony of the group. They rely on group dynamics, leverage rich information, and focus on substantive issues.

For Indian boards, it may be a long road to get there, but with the changing regulatory frameworks, oversights and demands from the minority shareholders, we expect the changes sooner rather than later. In Chapter 6 we discuss shareholder activism in detail.

References and further reading

Charan, R. (2011). Boards that Deliver: Advancing Corporate Governance from Compliance to Competitive Advantage (Vol. 20). Hoboken, NJ: John Wiley & Sons.

Desai (2014). Companies Act Series. Nishith Desai Associates. Available at: www.nishithdesai.com/information/research-and-articles/nda-hotline/companies-act-series.html. Last accessed 23 September 2015.

KPMG (2014). Companies Act 2013: Raising the Bar on Governance. KPMG. Available at: www.kpmg.com/IN/en/Documents/Companies_Act_2013_Raising_the_bar_on_Governance.pdf. Last accessed 23 September 2015.

MCA (2013). The Companies Act 2013. Ministry of Corporate Affairs. Available at www.mca.gov.in/Ministry/pdf/CompaniesAct2013.pdf. Last accessed 7 April 2019.

6 Shareholder activism and influence

**Case: governance malpractices at Infosys Ltd. and shareholders'
(founder's) activism**

On February 18, 2019, Bengaluru-based Infosys Ltd. settled a case with the
market regulator, the Securities and Exchange Board of India (SEBI), pertaining to the severance package of former CFO Rajiv Bansal, by paying
INR 3.44 million as consent fees to SEBI.

The background of the event goes back to April 2015, when the newly
appointed – and the first non-promoter – CEO of the company, Vishal
Sikka, made the decision to acquire two companies, Panaya and Skava,
for $200 million and $120 million respectively. The deals were questioned
by analysts for their merit and within a few months of the announcement
in October 2015, the then CFO Bansal resigned. Later, in May 2016,
Infosys disclosed that it had awarded over INR 170 million as severance
pay to Bansal. While earlier CFOs did not get similar severance
packages, Infosys claimed that this compensation to Bansal reflected his
"enhanced non-compete and non-disclosure agreement", without
divulging any further details.

The founder and first chairman of the company, N.R. Narayana Murthy,
became extremely critical in public forums about Infosys' decision to give
such a severance package and wondered if this was "hush money" paid to
Bansal to not talk about questionable acquisition decisions made by Sikka
and his team. The prolonged ugly public standoff between the founder and
the management not only led to Sikka's exit in 2017, but also saw the exit of
the then chairman, R. Seshasayee, and two other board members.

A follow-up investigation by SEBI found that Bansal's severance pay was
not in accordance with the remuneration policy; a related-party transaction
required the approval of the nomination and remuneration committee and
prior approval of the audit committee. Infosys had alsofailed to make detailed
and timely disclosures about the severance pay.

Eventually, Infosys filed a settlement application with SEBI in November
2017, where the company agreed to pay for a consent order, i.e. it paid a
negotiated penalty amount for its governance failures.

The theoretical perspective of shareholder activism

The concept of separating "ownership" and "control" and the relative dynamics of the two classes of entities (owners and managers) which form a part of either group leads to a peculiar situation (Black, 1992). The classical perspective of Berle and Means suggests that the "owner" shareholders are in a position to monitor the "controlling" management in two distinct ways – through the "voice" right and through the "exit" right. In other words, they may raise their voice of concern and they may also decide to exit the ownership when they observe unacceptable managerial practices (Nili, 2014). However, when shareholding is dispersed, the shareholders' incentive to monitor the management reduces, and the potential impact of the shareholders' "voice" is also reduced (Sridhar, 2016). In contrast, institutional shareholders, with a relatively higher concentration of holding, stand to gain significantly by exercising their "voice" right and thus tend to influence corporate governance practices in a positive manner (Sarkar & Sarkar, 2000). As large shareholders have substantial investments in the company, as well as significant voting power to protect these investments, they are likely to be more committed to a company in the long run, and they may be able to mitigate the collective action problem which could be present among smaller shareholders.

However, large shareholders, due to their influential position, may pursue specific individual gains that do not promote value-maximization for the firm. In this case, shareholder activism may be seen as a risk to the company. It is possible that activist shareholders pick up issues about which they have limited understanding, and their actions could adversely affect the management's work, and in turn negatively impact the valuation of the company. In addition, large shareholders may find it mutually beneficial to collude with the management for their own gain in a way that reduces firm value and hurts the interests of smaller shareholders (Sarkar & Sarkar, 2000).

Broadly, however, shareholder activism should not be seen as a cause for concern in improving corporate governance standards in companies. Through active interaction and involvement shareholders try to bring about a change that may or may not be supported by the management or the board. Such activities foster increased engagement of public shareholders with the company, making a company more efficient with higher capital productivity (InGovern, 2017).

The above theoretical and conceptual underpinnings have led to considerable review of shareholders' role, especially institutional investors' role, in monitoring, controlling and guiding the decisions of the management and the board in developed economies over decades. In the following section we explore how shareholder activism is taking shape in India.

Trends in shareholder activism in India

In line with global trends, the Indian market has been witnessing growing levels of advocacy by institutional shareholders. If we consider the resolutions voted against by institutional shareholders in companies listed in the NSE (see Table 6.1), the number has increased significantly in 2018 over prior years (NSEInfoBase, 2019).

The higher level of activism could be attributed to the mandatory introduction of e-voting facilities, greater role of proxy firms, and rising institutional holdings in several companies.

However, institutional shareholders' ability to stop resolutions is still weak, compared to that of the promoters. A detailed analysis of data published by NSEInfoBase (2019) shows that during 2018, the number of resolutions put up for voting in more than 1700 companies listed in the NSE has increased marginally to 12972 from 12341. The break-up of these by event-type is shown in Table 6.2.

Of the 12972 resolutions, based on available voting information, it can be inferred that promoters rarely vote against the resolutions, and when they do, their ability to stop the resolutions is stronger than the other two shareholder groups, i.e. institutional shareholders and public shareholders. On the other hand, while the institutional shareholders demonstrate maximum dissent, their ability to stop contentious resolutions is weak (see Table 6.3).

Table 6.1 Trend in institutional shareholders voting against resolutions

Year	2016	2017	2018
Number of resolutions where more than 20 per cent of institutional shareholders voted against the resolution	639	629	716

Table 6.2 Shareholder events and resolutions during Jan 2018 – Dec 2018

Event type	No. of events	No. of resolutions	No. of companies
AGM	1738	11520	1738
EGM	186	395	148
Postal ballot	477	980	395
Court / NCLT convened meetings	77	77	69

Table 6.3 Voting of resolutions by shareholder type

Voting of resolution by shareholder type	Promoters	Institutional shareholders	Other public shareholders
Number of resolutions, where voting details were available	9969	6822	10635
% of resolutions voted against (by more than 20 per cent)	0.31%	10.50%	3.97%
Success in stopping resolutions	25.81%	2.23%	4.98%

Support available for shareholder activism in the Indian environment

The Companies Act 2013 provides a range of support to shareholders to engage with the board and the management. Some of these are discussed here.

Shareholder approval: Under the act, several statutory matters require prior approval of a majority of shareholders, including related-party transactions, payment of non-compete fee, investments and borrowings beyond specified thresholds, executive remuneration beyond prescribed thresholds, sale of an undertaking of the company, amendment of the constitutional documents of the company, and issue of new shares.

Board involvement: Under the act, small shareholders can seek the appointment of a minority shareholder representative on the board of a listed company. Similarly, through an ordinary resolution directors can also be removed by shareholders.

Class action: The act grants shareholders the right to institute class action suits if they believe that the company's affairs are being conducted in a manner which is prejudicial against the interests of the company or its shareholders. Such a petition against a company would require the support of at least 100 shareholders or 10% of the total number of shareholders, whichever is lower, or any shareholder holding at least 10% of the shareholding of that company.

Call for a general meeting: According to the act, shareholders who collectively own 10% of the votes can require the board of directors to convene a general meeting of the shareholders.

Role of SEBI in addressing shareholders' concerns in listed companies

For shareholders of listed companies, SEBI's Listing Regulations provide additional rights and remedies. Under these regulations, each listed company is mandated to create a stakeholder's relationship committee, provide electronic voting facilities to shareholders, and disclose all material and pertinent information related to governance to all shareholders.

In 2011, SEBI commenced processing investor complaints in a centralized web-based complaints redressal system, called the SEBI Complaints Redress System (SCORES). Some of the key features of this system include maintaining a centralized database of all complaints, the electronic transfer of complaints to the concerned listed companies, online status / action-taken updates by all involved parties, and online viewing of a complaint's status by the complainant. The scope of complaints include issues that are covered under the SEBI Act, Securities Contract Regulation Act, Depositories Act and rules and regulations made therein, and relevant provisions of the Companies Act, 2013.

Table 6.4 provides a snapshot of the SCORES database (SCORES, 2019) for important categories of complaints and their resolution status as of the end of 2018. It is evident that SEBI has been able to provide a valuable service to investors on a range of issues.

Table 6.4 Processing of investor complaints in the SEBI complaints redress system (SCORES)

Issue category	Received	Pending actionable	Closure
Refund / allotment / dividend / transfer / bonus / rights / redemption / interest	107632	849	99%
Corporate governance / listing conditions	10693	147	99%
Mutual funds	22992	131	99%
Non-demat / remat	1622	99	94%
Prelisting / offer document (shares)	8730	80	99%
Takeover / restructuring	1402	33	98%
Delisting of securities	3420	33	99%
Buy back of securities	1052	24	98%
Prelisting / offer document (debentures and bonds)	680	11	98%
Collective investment scheme	13743	2	100%
Minimum public shareholding	138	1	99%
Accounting manipulation by listed companies	519	0	100%
Insider trading	1809	0	100%
Price / market manipulation	4909	0	100%

Keeping with global trends, shareholder activism – as empirical data shows – is on the rise in India. Thus, it is imperative for companies in India to adopt global best practices in engaging with the shareholders. Such engagements need not take place at the time of voting only, but they can be done through regular information dissemination and communication during the year, with necessary deliberations on the long-term strategic roadmap for the organization. These would ensure the shareholders, the management and the directors are all on the same page. In addition, companies need to constitute boards that secure the trust of the shareholders, leading to reduced suspicion and negative activism on the part of the shareholders.

References and further reading

Black, B. S. (1992). Institutional investors and corporate governance: The case for institutional voice. *Journal of Applied Corporate Finance*, 5(3), 19–32

InGovern (2017). *India Proxy Season 2017: An Analysis*. Available at: www.ingovern. com. Last accessed 16 February 2019.

Nili, Y. (2014). Missing the forest for the trees: A new approach to shareholder activism. *Harvard Business Law Review*, 4(1), 157.

NSEInfoBase (2019). *National Stock Exchange InfoBase Press Release: 2018 Witnesses Greater Advocacy by Institutional Shareholders*. Available at: http://www. nseinfobase.com/newsroom.aspx. Last accessed 16 February 2019.

Sarkar, J., & Sarkar, S. (2000). Large shareholder activism in corporate governance in developing countries: Evidence from India. *International Review of Finance*, 1(3), 161–194.

SCORES (2019). *Securities and Exchange Board of India (SEBI) Complaints Redress System*. Available at: https://scores.gov.in/scores/Welcome.html. Last accessed 16 February 2019.

Sridhar, I. (2016). Corporate governance and shareholder activism in India: Theoretical perspective. *Theoretical Economics Letters*, 6(4), 731.

Varottil, U. (2012). The advent of shareholder activism in India. *Journal on Governance*, 1(6). Available at: http://dx.doi.org/10.2139/ssrn.2165162. Last accessed 19 April 2019.

7 Corporate governance in public sector enterprises

Case: Coal India and The Children's Investment (TCI) Fund

In 2010, the Indian government sold a 10 per cent stake in Coal India Limited (CIL), one of the largest state-owned enterprises in India, for $3.4 billion in the country's largest ever IPO. UK-based institutional investor, The Children's Investment Fund Management (TCI), picked up a stake of as much as 1.8 per cent in the company during this IPO. This stake purchase made TCI the largest institutional shareholder in the company.

In 2011 TCI threatened legal action against Coal India's directors for not protecting minority shareholder interests. TCI claimed that Coal India's directors were acting against the interests of stakeholders by "blindly" accepting government instructions on the pricing of coal, reducing the profitability of the company.

Coal India, which produces nearly 80 per cent of all coal in India, bowed to pressure from the government and reversed a price increase after protests by power producers struggling with domestic coal supply shortages. Coal India also signed fuel supply agreements with power producers, guaranteeing to supply 80 per cent of contracted quantity at lower price points.

In 2012, TCI filed lawsuits in the Calcutta and Delhi High Courts against the chairman and directors of Coal India for alleged mismanagement that cost the firm more than INR 20 billion. TCI wanted an injunction on the powers of the board of directors that would restrain them from taking any decision which – according to TCI – was detrimental to the profitability of the company. The petitions had even named the Union government as a party for abusing its powers as a majority stakeholder in Coal India.

Oscar Veldhuijzen, partner at TCI, mentioned to the press at that time: "We have brought this claim reluctantly and only after repeated futile attempts to engage with the CIL directors. CIL has huge potential but none of that will be realized until its directors do their jobs properly. We remain a willing and constructive partner for CIL but they need to stand up to the Ministry of Coal and act in the interests of their shareholders."

Two years on in 2014, in an apparent disillusionment with the Indian system, including the response from the government on the issue, TCI withdrew the lawsuit against CIL. In parallel, it gradually lowered its stake in CIL, and exited the company by the end of 2014.

State owned enterprises: an overview

The Organization for Economic Cooperation and Development (OECD, 2018) defines State Owned Enterprises (SOEs) as the enterprises where the state (either federal or regional) has significant control through full, majority, or significant minority ownership. They are known by different names, such as government corporations, parastatals, public enterprises, or public sector units, and they take various legal forms. SOEs have been rising in influence in the global economy over the past decade. For instance, the proportion of SOEs among the Fortune^{TM} Global 500 grew from 9% in 2005 to 23% in 2014, including a greater presence in the top rankings. This increased SOE presence in the Global 500 has been driven primarily by Chinese SOEs, followed by Indian SOEs (PwC, 2015). The prevalence of SOEs also differs across sectors, with resources, utilities, and financial services as dominant sectors in the Fortune Global 500 SOEs.

The World Bank has defined a set of common purposes for state ownership in the production and delivery of goods and services (World Bank, 2006). SOEs might provide essential public goods and services that are required by all citizens; they improve labour relations, particularly in "strategic" sectors; SOEs limit private and foreign control in the domestic economy, generate public funds, and increase access to public services. In addition, they encourage economic development and industrialization through sustaining sectors of special interest for the economy, launching new and emerging industries by investing large quantities of capital, and controlling the decline of sunset industries, with the state receiving ownership stakes as part of enterprise restructuring. Often governments have created and invested in SOEs because markets were imperfect or unable to accomplish critical societal needs such as effectively mobilizing capital or building enabling infrastructure for economic development, e.g. a nationwide electricity grid or water system.

Once these goals are fulfilled and the domestic market matures, the question arises: what is their new purpose? Should they be privatized and corporatized? If they are to be taken out of complete government ownership, should they be fully privatized or should they be operated in a mixed model?

SOEs have become tools for countries such as China and India to position themselves better for the future in the global economy, and most of the SOEs from these countries are growing larger over time. However, there is a general downward trend in state ownership, with a tendency for the governments to divest their ownership stakes partially or fully. A partial dilution of stake means that while there may be a drop in the share of SOEs in a national economy, this does not necessarily equate to a corresponding decrease in the government's ability to wield influence over these enterprises.

Recent developments to maximize returns on assets, particularly for countries needing to reduce fiscal deficits and public debts, have led to stake sales by different governments. In Australia there has been a trend towards "capital recycling" which has further resulted in a wave of SOE asset sales to free up funds for reinvestment into much needed infrastructure such as major road projects (PwC, 2015).

At the time of India's independence in 1947, SOEs were perceived to be the best way to accelerate the growth of core sectors of the economy given a weak industrial base, inadequate infrastructure, lack of skilled human capital and an underdeveloped private sector. However, when the Indian market re-opened to foreign investors in 1991, the country underwent only partial privatization of its SOEs instead of complete divestment of state holdings.

As India's economy has matured in the past seven decades, both the privately owned enterprises (POEs) and SOEs have developed and flourished over time. However, reports highlight several challenges with India's SOEs, despite their significant contribution to the Indian economy. While policymakers have adopted disinvestments over the past two decades as the primary mechanism to reduce liabilities and improve SOE performance, it needs to be seen how SOEs fare in comparison to their private counterparts. In addition, we do not know how corporatization and other firm-level factors contribute to superior performance in SOEs. This chapter carries out a comparative investigation of the long-term performance trend of Indian SOEs vs. POEs from similar industries, and attempts to identify the factors that drive superior performance in Indian SOEs.

Genesis of Indian SOEs

In 1947 India became independent as a vast, poor nation with limited infrastructure, social unrest, and mass illiteracy. In order to develop the new fabric of Indian society, economic development became the prime objective of Indian policymakers post independence. They had to decide on an industrial policy that would address the development strategy for the future, and policymakers saw the need to set up the SOEs. SOEs were expected to develop infrastructure, catapult the economic activities of the nation, create jobs, and also provide stimuli to private sector businesses, and thus make India a mixed economy.

Recognizing the need for government control and direction in the initial days, the first Industrial Policy of 1948 reserved "core industries" for the SOEs, whereas "non-core industries" would be open to both public and private players. However, as Misra and Puri (2014) observe, over the next several decades, the SOEs were often preferred over private enterprises to achieve the goals of public policy. Some of the key reasons for this are listed below.

1 **Constitutional provisions and state controls**: The Constitution of India directed the state "that the ownership and control of the material resources of the community are so distributed as best to subserve the common good" and that "the operation of the economic system does not result in the concentration of wealth and means of production to the common detriment". (https://mhrd.gov.in/directive_principles_of_state_policy_article-39) In addition, in the strategic and core sectors of industry, the government wanted to keep ownership and control in its hands to shape the economic development of the nation.

2 **Development of infrastructure, removal of regional disparities and income inequalities**: India's colonial past had hindered comprehensive development of infrastructure across the nation and SOEs were expected to correct it.

3 **Long gestation period and risks**: Certain basic and heavy industries which were highly capital-intensive and had long gestation periods before giving returns, such as steel, fertilizers, and chemicals, remained in the hands of SOEs for decades.

Concomitantly, during the first five decades after independence, the central government and state governments set up several SOEs in both core and noncore sectors. In addition, the governments nationalized and consolidated several privately owned organizations to create large SOEs within the country.

However, by the end of the 1980s the controlled business environment in the country and the globalization phenomenon across the world started impacting Indian industries and companies, especially the SOEs. Superior products from across the borders, emerging technologies, lack of capital investments, and an absence of operational excellence took a toll at the organization level, which manifested at the macro-level. The nation witnessed the clichéd "Hindu rate of growth" of three per cent between 1951 and 1991. By then the inefficient SOEs had become and were continuing to be a drag on the government's resources, turning themselves into liabilities. Profitability was low due to pricing policies, underutilization of capacity, planning and implementation issues with projects, labour problems, and lack of autonomy. Low returns from SOEs were also adversely affecting the national gross domestic product and gross national savings. Around the same time, with impetus from globalization and the opening up of capital markets, many Indian POEs grew significantly to establish themselves as key players in different industries.

The government made a distinct shift in its position in 1991 with its industrial policy. The new policy argued for maintaining sustained growth in productivity, enhancing gainful employment, and achieving optimal utilization of human resources to attain international competitiveness, and to transform India into a major partner and player in the global arena. The economic reforms that followed included the abolition of industrial licensing for most industries, and allowing foreign direct investment (FDI) of up to 51 per cent equity in high-priority industries that required large investments and advanced technology. In addition, the restructuring of SOEs through disinvestments was expected to address their low productivity, over-staffing, lack of technological upgradation and low rate of return.

However, it is worth noting that the downturn in SOE performance was not uniform across the spectrum. While some SOEs suffered demonstrably poor results, many successful Indian SOEs, riding new opportunities, became giant global corporations, with a growing international presence. These profitable, successful SOEs were later termed "Maharatna", "Navaratna" and "Miniratna", i.e. jewels of the nation, classified under three categories.

Consequently, the government took a view to getting rid of the loss-making units, to concentrate on select core activities and raise funds to meet its fiscal needs by divesting stakes in these SOEs. By corporatizing profit-making SOEs through partial disinvestments without losing their controlling stake, the government was in a position to generate much-needed capital to address its growing fiscal deficits. Towards this, the government adopted the "Disinvestment policy" as an active tool to reduce the burden of financing the SOEs. The main objectives of disinvestment were: (a) to reduce the financial burden on the government; (b) to improve public finances; (c) to introduce competition and market discipline; (d) to fund growth; (e) to encourage a wider share of ownership; and (f) to depoliticize non-essential services. As per information available from the government, the 52 central SOEs that are listed in stock exchanges had a total market capitalization of INR 15.2 trillion at the end of fiscal year 2018 (GoI, 2019), and the government held a majority stake in all these SOEs. Appropriate and further disinvestment could help in generating funds for financing the increasing fiscal deficit, financing large-scale infrastructure development, retiring government debt, spending for social programs like health and education, etc.

Disinvestment is also significant due to the prevalence of an increasingly competitive environment, which makes it difficult for many SOEs to operate profitably. Losses in SOEs lead to rapid erosion of the value of public assets, making it critical to disinvest early to realize a higher value. Corporatization has not only brought improved governance and oversight to these SOEs, but it has also ensured that they operate in a mixed model – taking care of nation building as well as compete with their private counterparts in the marketplace, focusing on operational excellence. In addition, periodic stake sales and annual dividends from profitable SOEs are a major source of income for the government.

India's experiment and experience with development strategies is an interesting study. With the opening up of the economy, promotion of industry-friendly policies, and disinvestment in SOEs, the economy clocked a growth rate of eight per cent and above in the early 2000s, which subsequently stabilized at around seven per cent after the economic meltdown of 2008.

Theory of SOEs

Peng et al. (2016) posit that the rich set of theories developed over decades on firms and organizations essentially assume that firms are privately owned enterprises. SOEs, despite their large impact on the world economy, have not seen theory contextualized in a manner that addresses their uniqueness. Though SOEs at one time were predicted to disappear from the economic landscape of the world, today SOEs in some developing nations are growing to become prevalent in the world economy. Drawing on a large set of cases across industries and countries, Bruton et al. (2015) argue that today's SOEs are essentially a set of hybrid organizations, with elements of state ownership and control on one hand and private participation on the other. In such a hybrid organization, the primary owner, i.e. the government, is responsible for balancing competing economic, political, and financial objectives (Megginson & Netter, 2001).

This adaptive and enduring organizational form generates as much as 10% of global GDP and represents some of the world's largest firms.

There are two explanations for the existence of SOEs: the first is economic, and centres on the solution of market imperfections, and the second is political, centring on the ideology and political strategy of government officials regarding the private ownership of particular productive assets. Peng et al. (2016) explain these factors by extending the following core theories.

Perspective of property rights and agency theory

The property rights of an SOE can be broken down into three elements: rights to income generated from the property, rights to control and use of the property, and rights to transfer or sell the property. A government-owned organization essentially belongs to all the citizens of the nation, but almost all controlling rights belong to bureaucrats in the ministry owning the SOE. The question is how these rights influence the performance of SOEs. Considering the tenets of capitalism that form the basis of private organizations, it can be argued that when incentives to innovate are weak, imperatives to contain costs are moderate, and performance criteria are more long-term and non-economically oriented, private firms may be outperformed by SOEs. However, when incentives to innovate are strong, imperatives to contain costs are compelling, and performance criteria are more short-term and economically oriented, private firms will outperform SOEs. In addition, as the state is the de facto owner and SOE employees are the agents working for the state, the conflicts of interest between principals and agents become highly relevant. Incentive problems may not sufficiently motivate SOE managers and employees to strive for a high level of economic performance. State owners (principals) of SOEs are likely to experience monitoring problems that lead to SOEs' deviation from state owners' goals.

Transaction cost theory

We know from transaction cost theory that firms exist to economize on transaction costs in a more efficient way than markets can. Extending this logic, SOEs, despite their imperfections, exist to economize on transaction costs in a more efficient way than markets can. Therefore, in underdeveloped economies that observe frequent market failures, SOEs are likely to arise. In addition, the boundaries of SOEs are determined by trade-offs between the transaction cost savings brought by state control and the additional bureaucratic costs brought by state agencies and units involved in the management of SOEs.

Resource-based theory

As an economic enterprise, the SOE has long been considered a collection of production resources and capabilities. While the resource-based theory has traditionally focused on market-based resources and capabilities, it can be extended to non-market-based political resources and capabilities. Therefore, it can be argued that – driven by their interest to enhance the value, rarity, and inimitability of resources and capabilities – SOEs are likely to develop and leverage non-market-based political ties – especially in industries with strong state influence. The economic performance of SOEs is likely to improve when they leverage both market-based competitive capabilities and non-market-based political capabilities.

Review of extant literature

Corporate governance, accounting, and the accountability in SOEs are crucial and growing topics in public management and other research disciplines. Grossi et al. (2015) find that public service provision and profit maximization cannot be realized effectively and efficiently without powerful governance and proper management of SOEs. The reasons behind poorer returns on capital in SOEs are weak corporate governance, inappropriate incentives at the SOEs, and limited access of private firms to stock equity. Such a return differential would imply that if the distortion to capital allocation were reduced, the massive national investment in SOEs could be reduced without affecting growth outcomes (Dollar and Wei, 2007).

SOEs and their respective governments have been pursuing corporatization and privatization to address performance, governance and growth issues. Towards this, they tend to follow the model of private firms, with profit-seeking motives, obliterating their social goals. Empirical analysis shows that SOEs are found to be successful with their profitability goals as they go through corporatization (Bozec & Breton, 2003). In a recent meta-analysis of empirical studies, Bachiller (2017) finds that companies privatized by public offerings obtain a better performance than companies privatized using other methods, such as private sale or voucher privatization. He also establishes that privatization in developing countries does improve the financial performance of the organizations.

However, corporatization through stock market listing and the divesting of government stake alone may not bring performance gain or efficiency to SOEs. Shirley (1999) provides evidence from a sample of 12 developing countries, showing that the countries with improved SOE performance primarily followed a comprehensive strategy of reforms, including a combination of privatization and corporatization. Analysing the political economy of state enterprise reform, she finds that privatization and corporatization have similar political costs and tend to succeed or fail together. Where reform was politically desirable, feasible and credible, countries privatized and corporatized successfully, whereas in countries which were not politically ready to reform, alternative ownership strategies were not successful in improving performance. Similarly, Zhu (1999) argues that a mass corporatization drive by itself, without institutional underpinnings, is unlikely to solve the more fundamental agency problem, and that the key to successful restructuring of SOEs lies in the transformation of state ownership and the creation of effective governance mechanisms, which in turn requires the development of the country's market-oriented institutions.

Institutional development and quality of corporate governance also influence the acquisition performance and international expansion of SOEs (Lebedev et al., 2015; Liang et al. 2015). Some of the non-business arguments that explain the global expansion of SOEs are: (a) to benefit from achieving the political objectives of the home government; and (b) to find support for governments' diplomatic initiatives (Cuervo-Cazurra et al., 2014). Arocena and Oliveros (2012) analyse the impact of privatization of state-owned enterprises in Spain and find that the efficiency of these firms significantly improves after privatization.

Partial privatization, in which only non-controlling shares of firms are sold on the stock market, may be perceived as ineffective, as management control is not transferred to private owners. This perspective ignores the role that the stock market can play in monitoring and rewarding managerial performance even when the government remains the controlling owner.

In the context of emerging economies, which have some of the largest global SOEs, the best performing firms seem to be those that convert the gains from the previous, relationship-based phase into market-centred resources and capabilities (Peng, 2003; Li et al., 2006). Firms that fail to realize the passing of their time are likely to fall behind or go out of business. Market competitive pressure, formalized corporate governance, and less government control are found to promote market orientation of SOEs in the transitional period. Empirical studies examining privatization's effects in developing economies find that privatization yields improvements in the operating and financial performance of divested firms (Megginson & Sutter, 2006), with positive post-privatization changes in output, efficiency, profitability, capital investment spending and leverage. Such gains are further extended in countries providing greater shareholder rights, in regulated industries, and in firms that restructure operations after privatization (Aiva-zian et al., 2005). Even without privatization, corporate governance reform is potentially an effective way of improving the performance of SOEs; such reforms represent a policy alternative for countries seeking to restructure SOEs without massive privatization. The results also suggest that it may be optimal for governments to carry out corporatization of SOEs before eventual privatization. However, the role of the state in macroeconomic planning remains crucial in India and China – two large, low-income economies. The deregulation of state-owned enterprises is one of the most obdurate hurdles faced by transition economies as they adopt neoliberal structural adjustment policies (Saez & Yang, 2001).

Empirical studies on Indian firms comparing financial performance of dis-invested and fully-owned SOEs based on ratios pertaining to the profitability, efficiency, leverage, liquidity and employee productivity show that disinvest-ment has played a significant role in enhancing the financial performance of disinvested SOEs compared to fully-owned SOEs in a majority of the para-meters (Chhibber & Majumdar, 1998; Majumdar, 1998; Gupta et al., 2011). Agency costs for mixed ownership models tend to be lower than that of the concentrated state owned firms because they operate in an open market facing the regulatory framework of a competitive environment (Locke & Duppati, 2014).

In addition to disinvestment, empirical data shows that performance gain in Indian SOEs is also achieved through complex corporate restructuring that requires broad political consensus, extensive stakeholder consultation and buy-in, an innovative framework to deal with organization-specific issues, and a transparent process for divestment with in-built safeguards (Bose, 2011).

While partial privatization is perceived as ineffective (Arocena & Oliveros, 2012), Gupta (2005) shows that partial privatization in Indian SOEs has a positive and highly significant impact on firm sales, profits, and labour productivity.

Arguing for establishing a competitive market as an alternative to privati-zation, Ramaswamy and Renforth (1996) find that while many tout for transfer of ownership from government to private hands for value maximiza-tion, an alternative approach – increasing competitive intensity through decontrol of restricted industries without changing ownership to private investors – is likely to provide considerable efficiency gains.

In summary, the above studies establish that partial privatization through stake sale and consequent corporate restructuring contribute to improve-ment in SOE performance. However, there is no evidence of whether these performance gains are on par with the performance of comparable POEs. It has also not been established how firm-level factors in SOEs, other than disinvestment – especially, corporate governance parameters – contribute to performance improvement in SOEs. Considering the critical role of SOEs in the Indian economy, it is imperative to obtain insights into these aspects to contribute to the theory of SOEs as well as help policymakers engage in disinvestment decisions. The following research questions are framed to address these research gaps.

Empirical analysis: research questions

The above discussion highlights the fact that SOEs are unique organizations, and traditional theories of the firm need further extensions to explain the platform in which SOEs operate as economic entities. While SOEs play a critical developmental role in India, governance, efficiency, and performance issues have dogged SOEs for decades. As explained earlier, the Indian government's primary approach over the past two decades has been to sell minority stakes and list the SOEs on stock markets. In other words, the government corporatizes the SOEs, captures value through partial disinvestment, opens up the organizations for professional leadership and management, and lets the organizations transform themselves towards operational excellence. However, questions remain on the effectiveness of this approach compared to complete government control or complete privatization. The specific questions which we would like to explore here are: (a) the long-term performance trend of Indian SOEs; (b) the difference in governance parameters between SOEs and POEs; and (c) how corporatization, and concomitant governance changes, contributes to SOEs' performance.

Performance trends in SOEs and comparison with POEs

The Indian economy has witnessed the growing importance of POEs over SOEs in the past two decades, while at the same time a few of the SOEs have become behemoths, turning themselves into emerging market multinationals. It is necessary to understand how SOEs, collectively, have transformed over time and recognize the root causes behind this change. Prior empirical studies also suggest that the organizational differences between SOEs and POEs – the nature of their ownership, planning and operational processes, and agency relations – play a role in the way they perform. Therefore, we investigate how the performance of SOEs is different from that of POEs, even when they operate under similar external factors.

Difference in corporate governance practices between SOEs and POEs

Governance issues have been identified as one of the key reasons for relatively poor SOE performance (Bozec & Breton, 2003; Dollar & Wei, 2007; Grossi et al., 2015). Selling minority stakes, listing in stock market and adopting corporate governance best practices are seen as influencing factors driving up SOE performance. As independent directors participate in SOE boards, it is expected that such diversity will lead to improved oversight and governance mechanisms (Das & Dey, 2016). Therefore we argue that improved governance mechanisms positively influence SOE performance. Towards this, we investigate how corporate governance parameters differ between SOEs and POEs.

Benefits SOEs gain from corporatization and improved corporate governance

Theoretically, listed SOEs are subject to the same market scrutiny and discipline as the private listed companies. Bhasa (2015) finds that the Indian government has realized that SOEs under complete government ownership are a drag on the economy and hence have engaged in privatization and sell-out efforts. He finds that Indian SOEs perform marginally better than their private counterparts do and that their better performance could be due to the oligopolistic conditions they operate in, and possibly because of their business age.

Using data from an extensive sample of more than 100 Indian firms (SOEs and POEs), Majumdar (1997) finds that older firms are found to be more productive and less profitable, whereas the larger firms are, conversely, found to be more profitable and less productive. These performance differences are explained through market-restricting industrial policies that have been followed in India for decades. Ahuja and Majumdar (1998), in a study of 68 Indian SOEs, find contradicting results. SOEs not only demonstrate significant and systematic variations in performance, but in the case of SOEs, size is positively associated with efficiency, and age has a negative association with efficiency. Further, economic liberalization and reforms through the sale of stakes, aimed at improving the performance of state-owned firms, have induced efficiency gains over time. Thus, we would like to investigate whether age and size positively influence SOE performance. In addition, a more important question for us is how the concentration of government ownership and parameters of corporate governance influence SOE performance.

Methodology and data sources

For trend analysis of SOE performance, we consider all central SOEs and their key financial performance measures over the period fiscal 2009 to fiscal 2018.

For the comparison between SOEs and POEs, and studying the role of corporate governance parameters on firm performance, we use the same dataset which was analysed in Chapter 4. A total of 200 large Indian SOEs and POEs listed in NSE's Nifty200 index are considered for empirical analysis where the SOEs have varying degree of government stakes in them. A period of 20 years, from fiscal 1999 to fiscal 2018, which witnessed significant growth in the Indian economy, has been considered for this study. This unbalanced panel data has 3,141 company-year records, out of which 613 company-year records belong to SOEs. The companies represent a wide range of sectors, from primary industries such as agriculture and mining, to secondary and tertiary industries such as manufacturing, banking, retail and information technology. The Centre for Monitoring Indian Economy's

(CMIE) Prowess database and annual reports of the companies have been used to retrieve all firm-level information, i.e. financial performance, stock market performance, ownership data, and board-level information.

Firm performance is a multi-dimensional measure (Das & Dey, 2016). It is argued that adoption of inappropriate performance indicators may inhibit innovation for the firms, leading to ossification, with emphasis on quantifiable aspects at the expense of unquantifiable aspects of performance (Fryer et al., 2009; Thiel & Leeuw, 2002). Other unintended side effects of choosing inappropriate indicators are conflicts between interest groups, the pursuit of narrow, local objectives by managers at the expense of larger organizational objectives, and measure fixation, with emphasis on measures of success rather than on the underlying objectives.

Therefore, this analysis does not investigate specific indicators adopted by different organizations, and limits the scope to common, standard indicators that are published officially or that can be computed from publicly available data. We evaluate firm performance through seven outcomes encompassing accounting performance of the firm, stock market performance, and returns to the shareholders. These are same as the ones referred to in Chapter 4.

As performance measures data are not normally distributed, non-parametric tests have been used to compare SOE performance with POE performance.

The second part of our analysis compares SOE corporate governance parameters measures with the corresponding parameters for POEs. An independent sample t-test is appropriate to test if there is significant difference between the two sets of parameters.

The third part of our analysis deals with establishing causality of SOE performance. We test the role of firm-level factors as well as corporate governance parameters in predicting SOE performance. This is tested through step-wise multivariate regression. The regression model corresponding to these four hypotheses is depicted as:

$$y = \alpha + \beta_1 x_1 + \cdots + \beta_p x_p + \varepsilon$$

where y represents one of the twelve annual performance outcome variables, x_1 through x_p represent the firm-level variables representing age, size, concentration of government ownership, corporate governance parameters, and control variables, α is the constant term, β_i is the coefficient of x_i, and ε is the error term.

Keeping in line with the analysis in Chapter 4, we use firm age, total assets size, industry type, promoters' stake and institutional non-promoters' stake as control variables. Following Das and Dey (2016), quality of corporate governance is measured through board structure and board activities. While a higher presence of independent directors on the board is expected to improve governance quality, a higher promoters' share is expected to dilute governance quality. In contrast, evidence suggests that non-promoter institutional shareholders play an active role in the governance aspect of firms; therefore, a higher percentage of non-promoter institutional shareholding should lead to improved corporate governance quality, leading to superior performance. The definitions of independent variables, dependent variables and control variables used in the regression analysis have been documented in Tables 4.1 through 4.3.

For variables that demonstrate a wide range of values across firms, e.g. income, assets, PAT, etc., we transform them by taking natural logarithms. In addition, as the firms come from different industry sectors, we use industry sector and financial year as the control variables for multivariate regression. We use Durbin-Watson statistics for each of the models to confirm the absence of auto-correlation.

Findings and discussions

The trend analysis of the collective performance of all central SOEs in India is shown in Table 7.1. The number of SOEs during the period 2009–2018 varied from 217 to 254, and on average about 72 per cent of them were profit-making. Total capital employed in the SOEs went up by nearly 200 per cent, while total revenue went up by just about 50 per cent. Similarly, we notice that the total net worth of all the SOEs doubled, while total net profit went up by about 50 per cent only. Another interesting observation about the trend is that the total dividend paid by all SOEs went up by as much as 300 per cent, and average dividend payout ratio increased by 100 per cent. The average debt-equity ratio also fell significantly over the 10-year period.

In summary, the trends suggest that valuation and capital investments in SOEs have gone up significantly; however, growth in business, in the top-line as well as in the bottom-line, is not commensurate to such investments and rise in valuation. This indicates several possibilities – the SOEs in general are not becoming efficient; there could be pricing pressure; and, as the opening case on Coal India suggests, the government may be influencing pricing decisions within SOEs to the firms' detriment.

It is also interesting to observe that even though the SOEs are becoming less profitable, the dividend payout has been rising, suggesting that the primary owner of the SOEs, i.e. the government, is reaping significant benefits from its ownership.

The dataset used for comparative analysis of firm-level data of large SOEs and POEs is constituted from a sample of companies that form the Nifty200 index. All available annualized data for the selected 200 organizations for financial years 1999 through 2018 have been considered for analysis. Tables 7.2 and 7.3 depict the comparison of performance outcome variables between two groups of companies, and the statistical significance of the differences evaluated through non-parametric testing.

Non-SOEs are significantly better in firm performance on return on net worth, return on assets, and return on capital employed. However, in terms of net margins as well as PBDITA, SOEs perform better than their counterparts. Annual growth of SOEs is significantly smaller than that of the other firms; however, on further investigation of the high standard deviation for other firms, we notice that some of these reported very high annual growth as they started their operations in their initial days of existence.

Table 7.1 Performance trend of Indian SOEs owned by the central government

Measure / FY=>	2008–09	2009–10	2010–11	2011–12	2012–13	2013–14	2014–15	2015–16	2016–17	2017–18
No. of operating central SOEs	213	217	220	225	230	234	236	244	257	257
Capital employed (INR mil.)		7,922,320	9,080,070	11,538,330	13,378,210	15,081,770	17,104,530	17,641,130	18,219,710	22,739,690
Total revenue (INR mil.)	12,722,190	13,096,390	14,705,690	18,046,140	19,656,380	20,373,180	20,563,360	18,332,740	20,335,450	21,380,690
Net worth (INR mil.)	5,831,440	6,529,930	7,094,980	7,761,620	8,509,210	9,266,630	9,625,180	10,668,850	10,799,530	11,085,950
Overall net profit (INR mil.)	838,670	922,030	921,290	982,460	1,283,740	1,149,810	1,282,950	1,028,660	1,142,390	1,254,980
Profit-making central SOEs (nos.)	158	157	158	161	151	164	159	164	175	184
Dividend (INR mil.)	255,010	332,230	357,000	426,270	497,030	651,150	565,270	685,830	781,290	765,780
Net revenue from operations to capital employed (%)	160.5	137.09	129.83	136.2	129.02	120.79	108.83	83.34	82.11	86.84
Net profit to capital employed (%)	10.59	10.15	7.98	7.34	7.62	7.5	5.61	5.61	5.87	5.65
Net profit to total revenue (%)	6.4	7.25	6.26	5.44	5.95	6.24	5.23	6.48	6.89	6.31
Net profit to net worth (%)	14.38	14.12	12.99	12.66	13.51	13.84	10.69	10.58	11.76	11.58
Dividend payout ratio (%)	30.41	36.03	38.75	43.39	43.23	50.75	54.95	60.03	62.26	59.65
Debt / equity ratio (times)	2.69	2.98	2.95	3.63	3.86	4.25	4.44	4.75	0.93	0.99

Table 7.2 Descriptive statistics of firm performance variables in SOEs and other firms

Variable	SOEs		Other firms	
	Mean	Std. deviation	Mean	Std. deviation
Return on net worth (%)	14.06	14.88	16.32	76.88
Return on total assets (%)	4.69	7.54	7.83	8.62
Return on capital employed (%)	5.65	76.82	12.56	15.51
Net profit margin (%)	8.38	18.46	6.66	62.24
PBDITA as % of total income (%)	41.83	34.26	29.22	32.33
YoY growth in revenue	0.16	0.68	22.16	676.88
Major corp restructuring	1.35	0.61	1.81	1.38
Dividend rate (%)	93.62	117.44	215.80	961.15
Yield (%)	2.52	2.28	1.84	2.48
Tobin's Q	0.74	0.69	2.00	3.50
Market cap / EV	-1.20	40.17	0.86	0.90
Alpha	0.14	0.36	0.31	0.44
Beta	1.14	0.37	0.95	0.39

In terms of major capital restructuring, SOEs on average have undergone fewer capital restructures in comparison to other companies. While average dividend rate is lower in SOEs, the variation in dividend rates is higher in other companies. In contrast, dividend yield is higher in SOEs, suggesting that with stock price as the reference, SOEs pay higher dividends to their shareholders. Tobin's Q is higher in other companies, though the variation in values is also higher. Similarly, on average, the ratio of market capitalization and enterprise value is negative for SOEs, indicating very low prices of companies' shares, while cash and cash equivalent in the companies are comparatively higher. While average alpha is lower in SOEs, average beta is higher, suggesting lower returns from SOEs stocks while the risks remained higher.

In Table 7.3 we document the results from the Mann-Whitney U test, a non-parametric test of comparison between SOE performance measures and corresponding performance measures in other companies. While net profit margin between these two groups of companies does not show statistically significant difference, all other performance measures show statistically significant difference at 99 per cent confidence level.

Continuing our comparative assessment, we compare the corporate governance parameters of SOEs with non-SOEs. Table 7.4 shows the means and standard deviation of 14 parameters that we identified in Chapter 4 as measures of corporate governance. In the table the value of 1 for state-owned-enterprise indicates SOEs, whereas the value of 0 represents other firms. The number of directors is higher in SOEs, with relatively higher variance. The average number of female directors at 0.7 in a total board size of more than

Table 7.3 Non-parametric test on performance variables – SOEs vs. others

Statistic	Return on net worth (%)	Return on total assets (%)	Return on capital employed (%)	Net profit margin (%)	PBDITA as % of total income (%)
Mann-Whitney U	573737.000	537362.000	624923.000	770475.500	672127.500
Wilcoxon W	751643.000	727398.000	810668.000	983353.500	3628223.500
Z	-5.714	-9.060	-3.913	-1.076	-5.964
Asymp. Sig. (2-tailed)	.000	.000	.000	.282	.000

Statistic	Growth in revenue	Major corp restructuring reported	Dividend rate (%)	Yield (%)	
Mann-Whitney U	628270.000	46748.500	607341.000	198597.500	
Wilcoxon W	839845.000	54876.500	791869.000	1134993.500	
Z	-7.673	-3.457	-2.726	-8.102	
Asymp. Sig. (2-tailed)	.000	.001	.006	.000	

Statistic	Tobin's Q	Market cap / EV	Alpha	Beta	
Mann-Whitney U	165599.000	244761.000	206674.000	191831.000	
Wilcoxon W	243809.000	323367.000	285280.000	1107812.000	
Z	-11.690	-2.864	-6.926	-8.605	
Asymp. Sig. (2-tailed)	.000	.004	.000	.000	

a. Grouping variable: Dummy_GCE

Table 7.4 Group statistics of corporate governance parameters

Variable	State-owned enterprise	N	Mean	Std. deviation	Std. error mean
Number of directors	0	2468	12.163	4.749	0.096
	1	673	15.437	7.413	0.286
Number of female directors	0	2468	0.603	0.855	0.017
	1	673	0.704	0.926	0.036
CEO duality	0	2468	0.281	0.449	0.009
	1	673	0.646	0.478	0.018
Number of executive directors	0	2468	2.629	2.013	0.041
	1	673	4.844	4.925	0.190
Number of promoter directors	0	2468	0.921	1.663	0.033
	1	673	0.241	1.021	0.039
Number of independent directors	0	2468	4.775	2.935	0.059
	1	673	4.065	3.440	0.133
Total no. of board meetings reported	0	2468	3.966	2.196	0.044
	1	673	4.562	2.005	0.077
Directors' presence in board meetings	0	2046	0.646	0.129	0.003
	1	625	0.584	0.119	0.005
Independent directors' presence in board meetings	0	1983	0.735	0.160	0.004
	1	472	0.637	0.205	0.009
Directors' presence in other boards	0	2468	44.128	37.176	0.748
	1	673	28.632	21.269	0.820
Directors' average remuneration	0	2034	9539234.888	17124152.768	379693.899
	1	553	881906.793	789377.877	33567.762
Independent directors' average remuneration	0	1841	1336010.035	5401803.333	125895.983
	1	353	261621.621	265181.357	14114.180
Directors' presence in committees	0	1904	0.257	0.093	0.002
	1	503	0.253	0.129	0.006
Independent directors' presence in committees	0	1862	0.406	0.163	0.004
	1	400	0.357	0.205	0.010

15 shows insignificant presence of female directors on the boards. CEO duality is very high in SOEs, with more than 64 per cent of SOE boards demonstrating such duality. The average number of executive directors in SOEs is also higher compared to the average in other companies. In contrast, promoter directors have a higher presence in non-SOEs. While the number of board meetings is higher in SOEs, directors' presence, as well as independent directors' presence, in board meetings is lower. Directors' presence on other boards is significantly lower in SOEs, suggesting that SOE directors have limited insights into the functioning of other boards, compared to their

counterparts in non-SOE companies. Additionally, SOE directors are paid significantly less than their counterparts in non-SOE companies. Directors' participation in committees does not differ between these two groups. However, independent directors in non-SOEs participate more in board-level committees, compared to their counterparts in SOEs.

As the corporate governance parameters are normally distributed, we conduct t-tests to evaluate statistical significance of the differences in these parameters between SOEs and non-SOEs. The results of the independent sample t-tests are shown in Table 7.5. Directors' presence in board-level committees is not significantly different across the two groups. Presence of female directors is statistically significant at 95 per cent confidence level. All other parameters are statistically significant at 99 per cent confidence level.

As the last element of our empirical assessment, we establish causality between corporate governance parameters and firm performance. OLS regression is used to predict the firm performance measures listed in Table 7.2 using the corporate governance parameters listed in Table 7.4. In order to control for the effects of firm-specific factors, control variables have been introduced in the regression model. Tables 7.6 and 7.7 provide the descriptive statistics of independent variables and control variables.

Analysing the summary data on control variables, we notice that SOEs are mature companies with an average age of more than 47 years, and they are large in terms of assets. The Government of India on average has a majority stake to the tune of over 65 per cent in SOEs, suggesting the government's continued tight control on the strategic directions of SOEs. In addition, non-promoter institutional shareholders own significant stakes in SOEs to the tune of more than 21 per cent, suggesting that such institutional shareholders may be able to influence board-level decisions.

The research questions on how SOEs gain from corporatization and improved corporate governance are assessed through 13 models, where each model has one of the firm performance parameters as the dependent variable, with the selected corporate governance parameters as independent variables. In line with the transformation carried out on governance parameters in Chapter 4, we transform governance parameters into scale variables with a range of [0, 1], and deploy step-wise multivariate regression. As the industry codes are categorical in nature, we convert them into nine dichotomous dummy variables for the purpose of the regression exercise. Consolidated outputs from step-wise multivariate regressions for models involving return on net worth, return on total assets, and return on capital employed are provided in Table 7.8. Results for models involving net profit margin, PBDITA as % of total income, and annual growth in revenue are depicted in Table 7.9; results for models involving number of major corporate restructuring, dividend rate, and dividend yield are depicted in Table 7.10; and results for models involving Tobin's Q, market capitalization / enterprise value, Jensen's alpha, and CAPM's beta are depicted in Table 7.11, for each of the annual performance outcome variables.

Table 7.5 t-test of corporate governance parameters – state-owned enterprises vs. others

Variables		Levene's test for equality of variances		t-test for equality of means		
		F	Sig.	t	df	Sig. (2-tailed)
Number of directors	Equal variances assumed	19.817	.000	-13.864	3139.000	0.000
	Equal variances not assumed			-10.866	828.011	0.000 **
Number of female directors	Equal variances assumed	4.407	.036	-2.678	3139.000	0.007
	Equal variances not assumed			-2.559	1005.886	0.011 *
CEO duality	Equal variances assumed	43.207	.000	-18.442	3139.000	0.000
	Equal variances not assumed			-17.795	1018.303	0.000 **
Number of executive directors	Equal variances assumed	95.298	.000	-17.595	3139.000	0.000
	Equal variances not assumed			-11.409	734.231	0.000 **
Number of promoter directors	Equal variances assumed	301.045	.000	10.108	3139.000	0.000
	Equal variances not assumed			13.170	1746.862	0.000 **
Number of independent directors	Equal variances assumed	48.344	.000	5.351	3139.000	0.000
	Equal variances not assumed			4.889	955.098	0.000 **
Total no. of board meetings reported	Equal variances assumed	4.144	.042	-6.357	3139.000	0.000
	Equal variances not assumed			-6.695	1149.957	0.000 **
Directors' presence in board meetings	Equal variances assumed	7.724	.005	10.729	2669.000	0.000 **
	Equal variances not assumed			11.200	1109.063	0.000
Independent directors' presence in board meetings	Equal variances assumed	59.771	.000	11.178	2453.000	0.000
	Equal variances not assumed			9.618	614.589	0.000 **

Table 7.5 (Cont.)

Variables		Levene's test for equality of variances		t-test for equality of means		
		F	Sig.	t	df	Sig. (2-tailed)
Directors' presence in other boards	Equal variances assumed	135.837	.000	10.361	3139.000	0.000
	Equal variances not assumed			13.961	1899.081	0.000 **
Directors' average remuneration	Equal variances assumed	167.298	.000	11.884	2585.000	0.000
	Equal variances not assumed			22.712	2064.439	0.000 **
Independent directors' average remuneration	Equal variances assumed	16.063	.000	3.735	2192.000	0.000
	Equal variances not assumed			8.481	1884.987	0.000 **
Directors' presence in committees	Equal variances assumed	81.913	.000	0.780	2405.000	0.435
	Equal variances not assumed			0.646	644.451	0.519
Independent directors' presence in committees	Equal variances assumed	33.720	.000	5.169	2260.000	0.000
	Equal variances not assumed			4.469	513.203	0.000 **

Table 7.6 Descriptive statistics of board structure, contribution, and compensation in SOEs (independent variables)

Variable	Mean	Std. deviation
Number of directors	15.44	7.41
Number of female directors	0.70	0.93
CEO duality	0.65	0.48
Number of executive directors	4.84	4.92
Number of promoter directors	0.24	1.02
Number of independent directors	4.07	3.44
Total no. of board meetings reported in financial year	4.56	2.01
Directors' presence in board meetings	0.58	0.12
Independent directors' presence in board meetings	0.64	0.21
Directors' presence in other boards	28.63	21.27
Directors' average remuneration (INR)	881,906.79	789,377.88
Independent directors' average remuneration (INR)	261,621.62	265,181.36
Directors' presence in committees	0.25	0.13
Independent directors' presence in committees	0.36	0.21

Table 7.7 Descriptive statistics of control variables in SOEs

Variable	Mean	Std. deviation
Financial year	-	-
Age in years	47.59	25.98
Size – log(assets)	11.93	2.76
Promoters' shares (%)	65.76	17.98
Non-promoter institutions' shares (%)	21.39	14.26
Industry type	-	-

As the results in Tables 7.8 through 7.11 show, an absence of CEO duality in SOEs positively influences net profit margin and PBDITA, though it appears to have a negative influence on return on total assets. The influence of promoters in the board has a positive impact on PBDITA. Primacy of independent directors in the board positively influences return on assets as well as return on capital employed. In addition, there is a significant positive influence of independent directors' presence in the board on net profit margin as well as PBDITA. While the presence of female directors negatively influences return on net worth, it also has a positive influence on CAPM's beta. Directors' presence in board meetings positively affects net profit margin and PBDITA. Directors' presence in other boards positively affects dividend rate

Table 7.8 Regression results for state-owned organizations – Models 1, 2 and 3

Regression summary	Model 1: Return on net worth (%)		Model 2: Return on total assets (%)		Model 3: Return on capital employed (%)	
Independent variables	Std. β	Sig	Std. β	Sig	Std. β	Sig
(Constant)		.000		.014		.868
Financial year	-.341	.000	-.129	.016	-.009	.877
Dummy_Ind1	.087	.445	-.002	.988	-.179	.156
Dummy_Ind2	.052	.526	-.205	.010	-.130	.154
Age	-.016	.824	-.179	.009	-.058	.454
Size – log(assets)	.054	.471	-.141	.054	-.007	.934
Promoters shares held (%)	-.193	.028	.107	.221	-.030	.763
Non-promoter institutions shares held (%)	-.134	.084	.113	.145	.036	.684
CEO Duality	.037	.507	-.112	.037 *	-.038	.535
Influence of promoter directors	.009	.858	.056	.249	.016	.768
Primacy of independent directors	-.040	.441	.132	.010 *	.122	.036 *
Presence of female directors	-.111	.027 *	-.043	.384	.033	.560
Index of director's presence in board meetings	.011	.827	-.002	.966	-.032	.569
Index of director's presence in other boards	.108	.058	.033	.555	.014	.825
Index of directors' remuneration	.092	.181	.214	.001 **	.139	.068
Index of directors' presence in committees	.158	.001 **	.111	.020 *	.036	.511
Adjusted R²	.194		.222		-.005	
ANOVA df (d1,d2)	(15,390)		(15,398)		(15,393)	
F-value and p-value	7.516; 0.000		8.841; 0.000		0.864; 0.605	

** Significant at 99%; * Significant at 95%

and Jensen's alpha, and it negatively affects PBDITA, and CAPM's beta. Directors' remuneration positively affects return on total assets, Tobin's Q, and Jensen's alpha, and it negatively affects PBDITA and CAPM's beta. Directors' presence in committees positively influences return on net worth, return on total assets, and Jensen's alpha.

The 13 performance models measure different elements of firm performance, using quality of corporate governance measures with eight independent variables, relating to board structure, participation, and compensation. In line with prior empirical studies, the ratio of independent directors in the board seems to have a positive impact on several annual performance outcomes, suggesting that independent directors are in a position to guide SOEs

Table 7.9 Regression results for state-owned organizations – Models 4, 5 and 6

Regression summary	Model 4: Net profit margin (%)		Model 5: PBDITA as % of total income (%)		Model 6: Growth in revenue	
Independent variables	Std. β	Sig	Std. β	Sig	Std. β	Sig
(Constant)		.444		.812		.000
Financial year	-.045	.431	-.006	.844	-.275	.000
Dummy_Ind1	-.088	.446	-.769	.000	-.058	.620
Dummy_Ind2	-.027	.746	.076	.097	-.039	.643
Age	-.201	.005	-.200	.000	-.092	.201
Size – log(assets)	.112	.147	.233	.000	.119	.124
Promoters shares held (%)	.042	.653	.047	.360	-.194	.040
Non-promoter institutions shares held (%)	-.080	.334	-.068	.131	-.100	.233
CEO Duality	.170	.003 **	.144	.000 **	.023	.686
Influence of promoter directors	.077	.133	.057	.044 *	.020	.698
Primacy of independent directors	.180	.001 **	.128	.000 **	.059	.272
Presence of female directors	-.096	.065	.022	.438	-.033	.532
Index of director's presence in board meetings	.137	.010 *	.059	.042 *	.023	.663
Index of director's presence in other boards	.029	.623	-.093	.004 **	-.089	.135
Index of directors' remuneration	-.090	.199	-.121	.002 **	-.048	.498
Index of directors' presence in committees	.044	.384	.013	.627	.037	.458
Adjusted R^2	.083		.723		.066	
ANOVA df (d1,d2)	(15,420)		(15,420)		(15,419)	
F-value and p-value	3.637; 0.000		76.728; 0.000		3.049; 0.000	

** Significant at 99%; * Significant at 95%

towards better performance. Directors' presence in board meetings is expected to contribute to superior performance, and we observe that SOEs' profitability does improve with increased participation from directors in board meetings. On similar lines, we observe that increased participation of directors' in board committees results in statistically superior firm performance, measured through return on net worth, return on total assets, and Jensen's alpha. The extant literature also argues that when the board members are involved in other companies' boards, they develop broader perspectives and thereby are in a position to guide their own company better. The results from this analysis show that SOEs where directors are also directors in other companies have higher Jensen's alpha and reduced CAPM beta, suggesting

Table 7.10 Regression results for state-owned organizations – Models 7, 8 and 9

Regression summary	Model 7: Major corp restructuring		Model 8: Dividend rate (%)		Model 9: Yield (%)	
Independent variables	Std. β	Sig	Std. β	Sig	Std. β	Sig
(Constant)		.367		.476		.003
Financial year	.133	.386	.033	.553	-.202	.003
Dummy_Ind1	.510	.215	.216	.060	.124	.374
Dummy_Ind2	.052	.832	.247	.003	.019	.882
Age	.305	.146	.123	.083	-.046	.572
Size – log(assets)	.332	.156	.239	.002	.065	.480
Promoters shares held (%)	-.058	.820	.246	.008	-.264	.006
Non-promoter institutions shares held (%)	-.076	.728	.205	.012	-.198	.017
CEO Duality	-.120	.451	.019	.739	.018	.792
Influence of promoter directors	-.118	.463	.010	.843	-.067	.302
Primacy of independent directors	.158	.319	-.044	.405	-.064	.346
Presence of female directors	-.078	.603	-.057	.268	-.061	.352
Index of director's presence in board meetings	.033	.793	-.038	.464	-.035	.593
Index of director's presence in other boards	.175	.289	.231	.000 **	.095	.178
Index of directors' remuneration	-.206	.328	.044	.521	.018	.834
Index of directors' presence in committees	.223	.076	.034	.484	.092	.127
Adjusted R^2	.003		.132		.079	
ANOVA df (d1,d2)	(15,71)		(15,406)		(15,282)	
F-value and p-value	1.015; 0.451		5.271; 0.000		2.704;0.001	

** Significant at 99%; * Significant at 95%

superior market returns and reduced volatility of the stock. In addition, such SOEs have better dividend-paying trends, though such higher dividends probably impact profitability negatively. Similarly, it is also argued in the literature that superior directors' remuneration leads to better governance and thus better performance. While we see multiple evidences for this argument, in increased return on assets, improved market valuation (as measured through Tobin's Q), better market returns, and reduced volatility, we also notice a negative influence of this factor on SOE profitability. This leads us to the conjecture that superior board remuneration does lead to superior value creation; however, SOEs do need to keep watch on operational efficiency.

Table 7.11 Regression results for state-owned organizations – Models 10, 11, 12 and 13

Regression summary	Model 10: market cap / EV		Model 11: Tobin's Q		Model 12: Alpha		Model 13: Beta	
Independent variables	Std. β	Sig	Std. β	Sig	Std. β	Sig	Std. β	Sig
(Constant)		.602		.395		.000		.000
Financial year	-.032	.642	-.048	.441	-.304	.000	.269	.000
Dummy_Ind1	-.445	.002	-.049	.709	.005	.971	.152	.135
Dummy_Ind2	-.385	.003	-.114	.304	.228	.047	.246	.007
Age	-.039	.639	-.442	.000	-.027	.717	.116	.051
Size - log(assets)	-.058	.538	-.265	.005	-.097	.251	.112	.098
Promoters shares held (%)	.061	.522	.366	.000	-.086	.318	.428	.000
Non-promoter institutions shares held (%)	.058	.487	.377	.000	-.023	.764	.050	.407
CEO duality	.128	.069	.010	.872	.018	.781	.036	.473
Influence of promoter directors	.028	.664	.037	.490	.102	.084	-.007	.884
Primacy of independent directors	.047	.487	-.031	.592	-.087	.156	-.019	.694
Presence of female directors	.038	.567	.089	.114	-.008	.893	.325	.000 **
Index of director's presence in board meetings	-.045	.498	-.006	.911	.038	.531	-.046	.336
Index of director's presence in other boards	-.047	.510	-.027	.671	.156	.015 *	-.146	.005 **
Index of directors' remuneration	.029	.737	.215	.005 **	.192	.016 *	-.348	.000 **
Index of directors' presence in committees	-.036	.553	-.098	.064	.144	.009 **	.068	.122
Adjusted R²	.062		.332		.235		.513	
ANOVA df (d1,d2)	(15,282)		(15,281)		(15,282)		(15,282)	
F-value and p-value	2.309; 0.004		10.823; 0.000		7.079; 0.000		21.891; 0.000	

** Significant at 99%; * Significant at 95%

In line with extant literature, the absence of CEO duality shows positive influence on return on assets. However, we also notice that in the current dataset CEO duality also positively influences profitability. This leaves us with no conclusive evidence on CEO duality in SOEs. This can be explained by the fact that SOEs are strongly guided by the policies of the respective government ministries under which they operate. Such bureaucratic influence leaves limited control with the MD or the chairperson, even if they are different individuals. Similarly, the presence of female directors on the board shows conflicting statistical results. However, considering the fact that the average number of female directors on SOE boards is about 0.7 (see Table 7.6), any statistical inference using such an insignificant number would be inappropriate.

Conclusion

In this chapter, we have attempted to understand the conceptual foundations of SOE formation and their objectives, specifically in the Indian context, and continued the empirical analysis. We have carried out: (a) trend analysis of SOEs' business operations; (b) comparison of performance between SOEs and non-SOEs; (c) analysis of the difference in corporate governance parameters between SOEs and non-SOEs; and (d) how corporate governance parameters influence SOE performance – from accounting perspectives, growth perspectives, and market perspectives.

SOEs in India have evolved over decades since India's first industrial policy was laid out in 1948. While POEs in India flourished and grew in the past three decades due to deregulation, opening up of the economy, expansion of capital markets etc., SOEs continue to play a significant role in the economy. Over the past three decades, the Government of India has sold a few SOEs to private players in non-critical sectors. However, the predominant policy has been controlled disinvestment, i.e. selling minority stakes in SOEs and listing them on stock markets. During this time, some of these SOEs have grown into very large, world-class corporations, especially those in the resources, utilities, and banking sectors where there is considerable government control. The Fortune 500 list of large global corporations for 2018 has seven Indian companies, and out of them four are Indian SOEs – namely, Indian Oil, ONGC, the State Bank of India, and Bharat Petroleum.

The trend analysis shows that the SOEs have grown in size over the past decade, though their ability to create value has come down. It is also interesting to note that SOEs are paying higher dividends, suggesting that the majority stakeholder, the government, may be benefiting from SOEs' business operations, while at the same time reducing SOEs' retained earnings, which could have been employed in business expansion. Supporting agency theory for SOEs (Peng et al., 2016), our findings also demonstrate that despite growth in most of the Indian SOEs, on average their performance is poorer than their counterparts in the private sector. This is true for accounting parameters, growth parameters, and market-related parameters, suggesting a general lack of focus on performance orientation and value creation as business entities.

We also find that higher presence of independent directors, directors' presence in board meetings, directors' presence in other companies' boards, directors' remuneration, and directors' participation in board-level committees positively influence one or more performance measures. This clearly suggests that SOEs with superior corporate governance parameters are in a position to create superior value as business entities.

It needs to be noted that irrespective of corporatization and better corporate governance practices, the memorandums of understanding (MoUs) agreed upon by the SOEs with their respective ministries also govern the way Indian SOEs perform and act. The tendency towards economic inefficiencies in SOEs is countered by the presence of these informal, non-contractual ties between a state bureaucracy and the SOE. These non-contractual ties generate mutually supportive interests between the government and the SOEs (Pingle, 1997). Such arrangements allow SOEs to access critical resources, receive government patronage, and in turn they are expected to provide rich dividend income to the government.

References and further reading

Ahuja, G., & Majumdar, S. K. (1998). An assessment of the performance of Indian state-owned enterprises. *Journal of Productivity Analysis*, 9(2), 113–132.

Aivazian, V. A., Ge, Y., & Qiu, J. (2005). Can corporatization improve the performance of state-owned enterprises even without privatization? *Journal of Corporate Finance*, 11(5), 791–808.

Arocena, P., & Oliveros, D. (2012). The efficiency of state-owned and privatized firms: Does ownership make a difference? *International Journal of Production Economics*, 140(1), 457–465.

Bachiller, P. (2017). A meta-analysis of the impact of privatization on firm performance. *Management Decision*, 55(1), 178–202.

Bhasa, M. P. (2015). Ownership structure and performance of listed state-owned enterprises vis-à-vis comparable private enterprises: Evidence from India. *IUP Journal of Corporate Governance*, 14(3), 7.

Bose, S. (2011). Restructuring state-owned enterprises of a state government of India: Problems, prospects, and lessons learnt. *Vikalpa*, 36(3), 47–60.

Bozec, R., & Breton, G. (2003). The impact of the corporatization process on the financial performance of Canadian state-owned enterprises. *International Journal of Public Sector Management*, 16(1), 27–47.

Bruton, G. D., Peng, M. W., Ahlstrom, D., Stan, C., & Xu, K. (2015). State-owned enterprises around the world as hybrid organizations. *Academy of Management Perspectives*, 29(1), 92–114.

Chhibber, P., & Majumdar, S. K. (1998). State as investor and state as owner: Consequences for firm performance in India. *Economic Development and Cultural Change*, 46(3), 561–580.

Cuervo-Cazurra, A., Inkpen, A., Musacchio, A., & Ramaswamy, K. (2014). Governments as owners: State-owned multinational companies. *Journal of International Business Studies*, 45(8), 919–942.

Das, A., & Dey, S. (2016). Role of corporate governance on firm performance: A study on large Indian corporations after implementation of Companies Act 2013. *Asian Journal of Business Ethics*, 5(1–2), 149–164.

Dollar, D., & Wei, S. J. (2007). Underutilized capital. *Finance and Development*, 44(2). Available at: www.imf.org/external/pubs/ft/fandd/2007/06/dollar.htm. Last accessed 19 May 2019.

Fryer, K., Antony, J., & Ogden, S. (2009). Performance management in the public sector. *International Journal of Public Sector Management*, 22(6), 478–498.

GoI (2019). *Public Enterprises Survey 2017–18*. Ministry of Heavy Industries and Public Enterprises, Government of India. Available at: https://dpe.gov.in/publication/pe-survey/pe-survey-report. Last accessed 19 May 2019.

Grossi, G., Papenfuß, U., & Tremblay, M. S. (2015). Corporate governance and accountability of state-owned enterprises: Relevance for science and society and interdisciplinary research perspectives. *International Journal of Public Sector Management*, 28(4–5), 274–285.

Gupta, N. (2005). Partial privatization and firm performance. *The Journal of Finance*, 60(2), 987–1015.

Gupta, S., Jain, P. K., & Yadav, S. S. (2011). Generating financial flexibility and financial performance through disinvestment: A comparative study of disinvested and non-disinvested public sector enterprises in India. *Global Journal of Flexible Systems Management*, 12(1/2), 27.

Lebedev, S., Peng, M. W., Xie, E., & Stevens, C. E. (2015). Mergers and acquisitions in and out of emerging economies. *Journal of World Business*, 50(4), 651–662.

Li, Y., Sun, Y., & Liu, Y. (2006). An empirical study of SOEs' market orientation in transitional China. *Asia Pacific Journal of Management*, 23(1), 93–113.

Liang, H., Ren, B., & Sun, S. L. (2015). An anatomy of state control in the globalization of state-owned enterprises. *Journal of International Business Studies*, 46(2), 223–240.

Locke, S., & Duppati, G. (2014). Agency costs and corporate governance mechanisms in Indian state-owned companies and privately owned companies: A panel data analysis. *Corporate Ownership & Control*, 11(4), 8–17.

Majumdar, S. K. (1997). The impact of size and age on firm-level performance: Some evidence from India. *Review of Industrial Organization*, 12(2), 231–241.

Majumdar, S. K. (1998). Assessing comparative efficiency of the state-owned mixed and private sectors in Indian industry. *Public Choice*, 96(1–2), 1–24.

Megginson, W. L., & Netter, J. M. (2001). From state to market: A survey of empirical studies on privatization. *Journal of Economic Literature*, 39(2), 321–389.

Megginson, W. L., & Sutter, N. L. (2006). Privatisation in developing countries. *Corporate Governance: An International Review*, 14(4), 234–265.

Misra, S. K., & Puri, V. K. (2014). *Indian Economy: Its Development Experience*. Mumbai: Himalaya Publishing House.

OECD (2018). *Ownership and Governance of State-Owned Enterprises: A Compendium of National Practices*. Organisation for Economic Cooperation and Development. Available at: www.oecd.org/corporate/ca/Ownership-and-Governance-of-State-Owned-Enterprises-A-Compendium-of-National-Practices.pdf. Last accessed 13 February 2018.

Peng, M. W. (2003). Institutional transitions and strategic choices. *Academy of Management Review*, 28(2), 275–296.

Peng, M. W., Bruton, G. D., Stan, C. V., & Huang, Y. (2016). Theories of the (state-owned) firm. *Asia Pacific Journal of Management*, 33(2), 293–317.

Pingle, V. (1997). Managing state-owned enterprises: Lessons from India. *International Journal of Sociology and Social Policy*, 17(7/8), 179–219.

PwC (2015). *State-Owned Enterprises: Catalysts for Public Value Creation?* Available at: www.pwc.com/gx/en/industries/government-public-services/public-sector-research-centre/publications/state-owned-enterprises.html. Last accessed 23 February 2017.

Ramaswamy, K., & Renforth, W. (1996). Competitive intensity and technical efficiency in public sector firms: Evidence from India. *International Journal of Public Sector Management*, 9(3), 4–17.

Saez, L., & Yang, J. (2001). The deregulation of state-owned enterprises in India and China. *Comparative Economic Studies*, 43(3), 69.

Shirley, M. M. (1999). Bureaucrats in business: The roles of privatization versus corporatization in state-owned enterprise reform. *World Development*, 27(1), 115–136.

Van Thiel, S., & Leeuw, F. L. (2002). The performance paradox in the public sector. *Public Performance & Management Review*, 25(3), 267–281.

World Bank (2006). *Held by the Visible Hand: The Challenge of SOE Corporate Governance for Emerging Markets.* The World Bank. Available at: http://docum ents.worldbank.org/curated/en/396071468158997475/Held-by-the-visible-hand-the-challenge-of-state-owned-enterprise-corporate-governance-for-emerging-markets. Last accessed 19 May 2019.

Zhu, T. (1999). China's corporatization drive: An evaluation and policy implications. *Contemporary Economic Policy,* 17(4), 530–539.

8 Governance and sustainability reporting in India

Case: business sustainability at ITC Ltd.

A conglomerate business house in existence since 1910, ITC is one of India's foremost private sector companies with a market capitalisation of about INR 3.5 trillion and a gross sales value of nearly INR 700 billion at the end of fiscal 2018. ITC's business operations are diversified – it has a significant presence in FMCG, hotels, papers, packaging, and agri-business. ITC is one of the very few Indian companies that has been publishing its sustainability report consistently, since 2004. According to the information on its website, ITC is the only company in the world, of its size and diversity, to be carbon, water and solid waste recycling positive. In addition, it is believed that ITC's diverse value chains create sustainable livelihoods for more than 6 million people, a majority of them in rural India.

It is interesting to note that ITC's long-term focus on sustainability, especially the attention its leadership team devotes to the issue of business sustainability, has reaped significant gains for ITC's stakeholders. Some of the key players in framing, reviewing and reporting ITC's sustainability practices include their Sustainability Compliance Review Committee (SCRC) of the Corporate Management Committee (CMC), and business unit chief executives. The 2018 sustainability report from the company (ITC, 2018) deliberates on ITC's sustainable supply chain, stakeholder engagement, corporate governance, economic performance, environmental performance, people and safety performance, social performance, and product responsibility. The document provides deep insights to ITC's stakeholders into the thought processes of the management, and provides key information on the company's economic and non-economic performance measures, process enhancements and adaptation of business models.

An active practitioner of business sustainability and a probable role model for many other Indian organizations, ITC's apparent success comes from its methodical approach to business sustainability which is evident from a series of sustainability-related policies ITC has developed. Some of these policies are discussed below in brief.

ITC's policy on lifecycle sustainability: According to this policy, ITC attempts to embed the principles of sustainability into different stages of the product or service lifecycle, including the procurement of raw material or a service, the manufacturing of a product or delivery of service, the transportation of raw materials and finished goods, and disposal by consumers. Towards this ITC ensures that its products and services comply with all regulatory norms, that the lifecycle value chain activities are ethical, that they do not violate any regulations, and that the processes are continuously enhanced to improve the balance between social, economic, and environmental impacts. In addition, ITC takes the responsibility to raise awareness among consumers of the responsible disposal of products and packaging.

ITC's policy on stakeholder engagement: ITC believes that inclusive growth is achievable through an effective stakeholder engagement process. ITC's stakeholder engagement relies on taking prioritized consideration of the economic, environmental and social impacts of its business on its stakeholders, understanding stakeholders' concerns and expectations, and responding coherently and quickly on stakeholder issues.

ITC's policy on responsible advocacy: ITC believes that it may need to play an advocacy role with policymakers and external stakeholders. Such engagement with the relevant authorities is guided by ITC's core values of ethics, commitment, integrity, and transparency, and in addition – according to the policy – its advocacy programmes need to balance the interests of diverse stakeholders.

Apart from these three, ITC's sustainability-related policies include policies on product responsibility, responsible sourcing, freedom of association, diversity and equal opportunity, prohibition of child labour and prevention of forced labour at the workplace, human rights consideration of stakeholders beyond the workplace, and policy on environment, health and safety (EHS).

The governance processes at ITC reinforce the company's commitment to ethical corporate citizenship and the company's aspiration to create enduring value for its stakeholders. During the period 2004–2018, as ITC continuously worked on sustainability, it grew its market capitalization by more than 1200 per cent, while at the same time transforming the lives and landscape of a large part of the country.

Superior governance: from compliance to business sustainability

Apart from ensuring regulatory compliance, superior corporate governance also involves managing business risks and sustained value creation through the creation of a business trajectory that involves adaptation and innovation. The board and leadership play an important role in charting this path of business sustainability. While business sustainability is normally perceived as managing the triple bottom-line (TBL) – profit, people, and planet – business sustainability in reality involves creating and evolving a resilient business model. The key activities involved in ensuring business sustainability are: (a) engaging with the stakeholders – learning from customers, suppliers, business partners, employees, and the extended community – to establish two-way communication and facilitate collaborative decision-making; (b) establishing environmental management systems – creating mechanisms within the organization and the value chain to embed environmental efficiency in business processes – so that the negative impact of business operations reduces; (c) conducting lifecycle analysis – systematically analysing the environmental and social impact of the products and services the organization uses and produces throughout the value chain – to identify opportunities to reduce, recycle and reuse, and introduce circular economy concepts in the business model; and (d) reporting and disclosure – measuring, controlling and reporting on an array of operational parameters to all stakeholders – to bring in transparency in communication to all stakeholders about sustainable practices adopted by the organization.

The above-mentioned activities lead to several short-term and long-term outcomes. In the short-term, the firm may experience an increase in costs of operations. However, in the long-term, the firm experiences a robustness of business model, growth in revenue and superior value creation, and intangible gains like superior reputation, recognized as a business partner of choice, customer loyalty, and a motivated workforce with a sense of purpose.

Over the past two decades, businesses around the world have witnessed the emergence of guidelines and standards to account for the social and environmental impacts of their operations. Though these standards are voluntary in nature, there is indirect pressure on firms from shareholders as well as larger stakeholder communities to adopt them (Vigneau, Humphreys & Moon, 2015). One of the most prominent set of standards that has assumed importance across the globe is the Global Reporting Initiative (GRI) standards for sustainability reporting.

GRI intends to encourage dialogue between corporations and stakeholders through firms' disclosure of information on economic, social, governance, and environmental performance. It has developed norms to report on firms' management approaches to address social and environmental issues, supported by a series of performance indicators on social, environmental and economic performance (GRI, 2013). By providing non-binding reporting guidelines, the GRI aims at promoting organizational transparency and accountability as well as stakeholder engagement. As of 2018, more than 12,000 organizations in the world engage in regular reporting on sustainability disclosures using GRI's frameworks.[1]

While GRI's approach is centred on disclosure, the Circular Economy (CE) concept, a relatively newer idea, takes a wider perspective on the sustainability of businesses – it originates from the industrial ecology paradigm, and conceptualizes the integration of economic activity and environmental well-being in a sustainable way. CE can be defined as "an economic model wherein planning, resourcing, procurement, production and reprocessing are designed and managed, as both process and output, to maximize ecosystem functioning and human well-being" (Murray, Skene & Haynes, 2017). The "ReSOLVE" framework (EMF, 2015) proposes six measures to introduce CE into business environments: "Regenerate", "Share", "Optimize", "Loop", "Virtualize" and "Exchange". "Regenerate" refers to a shift towards renewable sources of input content and energy. "Share" refers to the possibility of a shared utilization of goods among users and maximization of resource use along the product lifecycle. "Optimize" involves improving products' and processes' efficiency, removing waste from production and the supply chain. "Loop" refers to closing production loops. "Virtualize" refers to dematerialization, i.e. the possibility of delivering utility as a service instead of a physical product. Lastly, "Exchange" refers to the use of innovative technologies and materials to enable more resource-efficient industrial processes (De Angelis, 2018). CE practices are also closely aligned with several sustainable development goals promoted by the United Nations (Schroeder, Anggraeni & Weber, 2019).

Though CE makes significant sense as a concept, considering the rising crunch on natural resources, practical implementations are fraught with operational challenges and questions on cost vs. benefits.

This chapter explores how firms' boards and leadership teams can transition their organizations from disclosure-oriented sustainability to business models that can provide the promised benefits of CE. We find that sustainability disclosures through frameworks such as GRI help firms improve awareness among stakeholders, and over time contribute to innovation in business models. However, the true benefits that CE provides cannot be obtained unless there is a transformation of business models and industry structure.

Background and research questions

The logic of the linear industrial business model – i.e. take-make-dispose – entails extraction of resources, manufacturing, consumption and subsequent discarding by the consumers. The underlying economic principles primarily focus on efficient allocation of resources in the market and do not take into account the limited and exhaustible nature of natural resources. This model, which has been in practice since the industrial revolution, not only leads to the depletion of natural resources, but also creates waste, uncontrolled energy consumption, and is an unviable socio-economic trend (De Angelis, 2018). Over the past few decades an ever-increasing number of organizations, their investors, international bodies, governments, and society at large are attempting to make business and economic operations more sustainable. Moreover, expectations that long-term profitability should go hand-in-hand with social justice and protecting the environment are gaining ground (GRI, 2013). In this section we discuss some critical extant research on the sustainability of business environments, the role of sustainability reporting, and the emergence of CE, and we frame our research questions around this.

Business model evolution and sustainability of business processes

Demil and Lecocq (2010) posit that business model evolution is a fine-tuning process that involves voluntary and emergent changes in and between permanently linked core components, and firm sustainability depends on anticipating and reacting to sequences of voluntary and emerging changes. Arguing on similar lines, Aras and Crowther (2009) suggest that instead of short-term focus on efficiency and cost-cutting, firms should recognize their value-creating activities and redefine their business processes as and when necessary. The role of external, secondary stakeholders is important here. Brennan and Merkl-Davies (2014) demonstrate that business organizations tend to adapt their business processes towards sustainable practices and concede to external, secondary stakeholders' demands when stakeholders leverage metaphors and rhetoric.

Based on empirical studies on the manufacturing industry, Hall and Wagner (2012) find that integrative actions of strategic decisions and environmental management do lead to the superior long-term performance of firms – from both economic and environmental perspectives. Such studies suggest that the critical element in adapting business processes lies in pursuing an integrative approach, which takes into consideration unexplored value creation opportunities, and involves the larger societal ecosystem in the business model. In order to develop sustainable business models, Bocken, Short, Rana and Evans (2013) propose a value-mapping tool which introduces three forms of value – value captured, missed / destroyed or wasted, and opportunity – and four major stakeholder groups – environment, society, customer, and network actors.

Sustainability reporting and GRI

GRI has become institutionalized as the most-adopted global framework for voluntary corporate environmental and social reporting. Corporate sustainability reporting frameworks such as GRI are expected to provide a complete and balanced picture of the sustainability performance of the organization. A sustainability report is expected to disclose an organization's impacts – be they positive or negative – on the environment, society and the economy (GRI, 2013).

However, as these reporting actions are usually voluntary, the reports are prone to interpretation, and sometimes even suspected of greenwashing (Fonseca, McAllister & Fitzpatrick, 2014; Hahn & Lülfs, 2014). It is also found that the transparency of sustainability reports differs by ownership, size, and region of the organization, and that the influence of certain groups of stakeholders such as customers, clients, and employees affect the contents of the reports (Fernandez-Feijoo, Romero & Ruiz, 2014). Extending this criticism further, Levy, Brown and De Jong (2010) observe that the evolution of the GRI framework itself has been constrained by the preferences and choices of larger, more powerful institutions from financial and capital markets, while relatively weaker societal groups such as NGOs have been relegated to limited roles.

Tracing the history of sustainability, Milne and Gray (2013) identify the concept of TBL as the core and dominant idea that lead to sustainability reporting and business engagement with sustainability. TBL incorporates an entity's economic, environmental and social performance indicators into its management and reporting processes, but in the process true concern for ecology is ignored. As a result, the TBL and the GRI are insufficient conditions for organizations contributing to sustaining the Earth's ecology, and they may instead reinforce business-as-usual and greater levels of unsustainability.

Arguing for the limited effectiveness of prevailing corporate sustainability reporting practices, researchers have explained these activities through theoretical frameworks such as signalling theory and legitimacy theory – the organizations send out indications to their stakeholders that they continually seek to operate within the bounds and norms set by the secondary stakeholders and the society. As voluntary sustainability reporting practices are subjected to contradictory societal and institutional forces, phenomena such as organizational hypocrisy and organizational façade limit the prospect of these activities (Cho, Laine, Roberts & Rodrigue, 2015). In addition, corporations adopt several communicative legitimization strategies, as reporting negative aspects endangers corporate legitimacy. Studying large multinational enterprises' GRI-based reporting, Hahn and Lülfs (2014) find that such legitimization strategies include: (a) marginalization, i.e. rendering negative aspects non-relevant or unimportant; (b) abstraction, i.e. generalizing negative aspects as being prevalent throughout a whole industry; (c) rationalization, i.e. highlighting other benefits or emphasizing some form of natural development; (d) authorization, i.e. referring to authorities; and (e) imprecise provision of measures.

Studying the GRI-based sustainability reporting of mining companies, Fonseca et al. (2014) recommend that worthwhile and meaningful sustainability reports should go beyond data definitions and formats, and concentrate on better understanding of the context, scales, long-term effects, interactions, trade-offs, and synergies between factors that contribute to the environmental impact of a company's business. While there are technical and behavioural barriers to work on such improvements, the consequences of continued ineffective sustainability reporting would be grave.

Research questions

Despite the limitations of GRI's sustainability reporting framework, extant research shows that it is the most acceptable available; meanwhile, adoption of CE-oriented business models is evident only in select economies. Thus, our attempt here is to develop an Indian perspective on how sustainability reporting has evolved across organizations and industries, and how this evolution of reporting behaviour is leading to the adoption of CE-oriented business models. Based on the above discussion, we intend to explore the following questions:

- Are sustainability reporting practices uniformly adopted by all types of organizations across industry sectors?
- Has the quality of disclosures in Indian organizations improved over time?
- Have improved sustainability reporting and disclosures enabled organizations to adapt their business models to implement CE concepts?

The following sections describe the model, statistical techniques, and the results from the tests carried out on extracted GRI data reported from India to answer these questions.

Data and methodology

We extract data from GRI's sustainability disclosure records to create our analysis dataset that contains information about participating organizations and their reporting trends. These participating organizations belong to all geographic / economic regions, and differ by size – while a significant number of them are multinational enterprises (MNEs), we do have a significant population of small and medium enterprises (SMEs) as well. In addition, there is significant spread in terms of the primary industry of these organizations. In total, we have 10,126 organizations from 40 nations, and we study their sustainability reporting practices over the 10-year period 2008–2017. The definition of the variables is listed in Table 8.1.

The statistical analysis used is a one-way multivariate analysis of variance (one-way MANOVA) which determines whether there are any differences between independent groups on more than one continuous dependent variable. MANOVA allows us to study the effect of categorical independent variables on continuous dependent variables and hence is suitable for our analysis. Apart from three independent categorical variables, we also test for interaction effects in our model as specified below.

Design: Intercept + Org type + Industry category + Org type * Industry category.

Before we conduct our tests using the General Linear Model (GLM), we check for MANOVA assumptions, i.e. linearity among all pairs of variables, normality and homogeneity of variances, and covariances of dependent variables.

Results

Results from the GLM analysis are shown in Tables 8.2 through 8.7. Table 8.2 provides the descriptive statistics of the dependent variables, split by independent variables. The results show that the MNEs' reporting consistency is on the higher side, whereas for the SMEs it is on the lower side. Similarly, services firms in India, many of which have global business footprints, have higher reporting consistency. GRI G4 level statistics provide different insights – SMEs are better adopters of

Table 8.1 Definition of variables used in empirical analysis

Variable name	Type	Definition / explanation
Org type	Independent, categorical	Type of organization participating in sustainability reporting practice. Possible values: MNE, large, SME, others.
Industry category	Independent, categorical	Category of the primary industry in which the reporting organization operates. Possible values: conglomerates, agriculture, extractive industries, manufacturing, services, others.
Reporting consistency	Dependent, scale	Indicates how consistently the reporting organization has been reporting on the GRI platform since it first reported. Calculated as (no. of times reported during 2008–2017) / (2017 - year first reported + 1).
GRI G4 level	Dependent, scale	Indicates the number of times the reporting organization reported at GRI G4 level.

GRI G4 level reporting. This indicates that the SMEs, when they decide to adopt sustainability reporting, start at the highest level of reporting, leading to a larger proportion of SMEs reporting at GRI G4 level.

Further analysis reveals the differences across organization types, and differences across industry sectors. Table 8.3 shows that there is a statistically significant difference in GRI reporting based on organization type, $F (4, 760) = 7.491$, $p < .0005$; Wilk's $\Lambda = 0.995$. Similar significant difference is observed for industry category of the reporting organization, $F (10, 760) = 6.294$, $p < .0005$; Wilk's $\Lambda = 0.999$. We also notice a significance of interaction effect of organization type and industry category.

To determine how the dependent variables differ for the independent variables, we need to look at the tests of between-subjects effects as presented in Table 8.4. We observe that organization type has a statistically significant effect on both reporting consistency ($F (2, 381) = 8.115$; $p < .0005$) and GRI G4 level ($F (2, 381) = 6.762$; $p < .0005$). Similarly, industry category of reporting organization has a statistically significant effect on both reporting consistency ($F (5, 381) = 6.148$; $p < .0005$) and GRI G4 level ($F (5, 381) = 6.572$; $p < .0005$). In addition, the interaction effect of organization type and industry category demonstrates significant effects.

We follow up these significant ANOVAs with Tukey's HSD post-hoc tests. Table 8.5 shows the post-hoc test for organization type and both the dependent variables, and Tables 8.6 and 8.7 show the post-hoc tests for industry category for each of the dependent variables.

Tukey's post-hoc test on organization type shows that mean scores for reporting consistency are statistically significantly different between different organization types ($p < .0005$ for all combinations). Similarly, mean GRI G4 level scores are statistically significantly different between different organization types ($p < .0005$ for all combinations).

Table 8.2 Descriptive statistics

Param.	Org type	Industry category	Mean	Std. dev.	N	Param.	Org type	Industry category	Mean	Std. dev.	N
Consistent reporting index	Large	Agriculture	.833	.289	3	GRI G4 level	Large	Agriculture	.33	.58	3
		Conglomerates	.767	.345	16			Conglomerates	.38	.50	16
		Extractive industries	.744	.309	27			Extractive industries	.37	.49	27
		Manufacturing	.757	.325	84			Manufacturing	.42	.50	84
		Others	.847	.267	21			Others	.24	.44	21
		Services	.901	.214	102			Services	.24	.43	102
		Total	.823	.285	253			Total	.32	.47	253
	MNE	Agriculture	.750	.354	2		MNE	Agriculture	.50	.71	2
		Conglomerates	.733	.294	6			Conglomerates	.17	.41	6
		Extractive industries	.917	.144	3			Extractive industries	.33	.58	3
		Manufacturing	.976	.094	45			Manufacturing	.18	.39	45
		Others	.969	.125	16			Others	.00	.00	16
		Services	.933	.185	43			Services	.07	.26	43
		Total	.941	.164	115			Total	.12	.33	115
	SME	Agriculture	.333	.	1		SME	Agriculture	1.00	.	1
		Extractive industries	.667	.382	3			Extractive industries	.67	.58	3
		Manufacturing	.442	.206	14			Manufacturing	1.00	.00	14
		Others	.333	.	1			Others	1.00	.	1
		Services	.903	.224	11			Services	.18	.40	11
		Total	.626	.313	30			Total	.67	.48	30
	Total	Agriculture	.722	.310	6		Total	Agriculture	.50	.55	6
		Conglomerates	.758	.325	22			Conglomerates	.32	.48	22
		Extractive industries	.752	.302	33			Extractive industries	.39	.50	33
		Manufacturing	.795	.303	143			Manufacturing	.40	.49	143
		Others	.885	.239	38			Others	.16	.37	38
		Services	.910	.207	156			Services	.19	.39	156
		Total	.842	.270	398			Total	.29	.45	398

Table 8.3 Multivariate tests – GLM

Effect		Value	F	Hypothesis df	Error df	Sig.
Intercept	Wilks' lambda	.914	313.683[a]	2.000	380.000	.000 **
Org type	Wilks' lambda	.995	7.491[a]	4.000	760.000	.000 **
Industry category	Wilks' lambda	.999	6.294[a]	10.000	760.000	.000 **
Org type* Industry category	Wilks' lambda	.998	2.482[a]	18.000	760.000	.001**

a. Exact statistic
Design: Intercept + Org type + Industry category + Org type * Industry category

Tukey's post-hoc test on organization type and reporting consistency shows that mean scores for reporting consistency are statistically significantly only in two combinations – between the services industry and extractive industry (p = 0.012), and between the services industry and manufacturing industry (p = 0.001).

Similarly, the post-hoc test on region and GRI G4 level shows that GRI G4 level scores are statistically significantly different only between the services industry and manufacturing industry, and the services industry and other industries.

Our first research question, whether sustainability reporting practices are adopted across organization types and industry sectors uniformly, has found partial support. While the descriptive statistics indicate adoption of the GRI reporting framework and GRI G4 level reporting across all types of organization, there is significant difference in intensity of adoption across organization types and some industry sectors.

To test our second hypothesis, we take a longitudinal view of our dataset by year, as depicted in Table 8.8, providing a comparison of trends in GRI G4 adoption between India and global levels. We notice that since its introduction in 2013, an increasing number of companies are adopting the rigorous and objective GRI G4 level reporting, except for in the 2017. In addition, its adoption level in India is faster than its adoption level globally. This suggests that the top management teams, including the boards, of progressive Indian companies recognize the importance of sustainability reporting, and most of them are willing to adopt more comprehensive standards such as GRI G4 ahead of the rest of the world. In 2016, about 34 per cent of all sustainability reports published by organizations globally followed GRI G4 standards, while in India the corresponding number was 54 per cent. Thus, we conclude that Indian firms have improved in their quality of disclosure.

However, data from the GRI database also indicates that reporting volume under GRI G4 standards came down globally in 2017. This anomaly may be explained by the fact that several companies had yet to report their 2017 sustainability performance when the data was collected from the GRI repository.

Table 8.4 Tests of between-subjects effects – GLM

Source	Dependent variable	Type III sum of squares	df	Mean square	F	Sig.
Corrected model	Reporting consistency	5.736[a]	16	.359	5.865	.000 **
	GRI G4 level	14.808[b]	16	.925	5.266	.000 **
Intercept	Reporting consistency	34.977	1	34.977	572.230	.000 **
	GRI G4 level	11.890	1	11.890	67.650	.000 **
Org type	Reporting consistency	.992	2	.496	8.115	.000 **
	GRI G4 level	2.377	2	1.188	6.762	.001 **
Industry category	Reporting consistency	1.879	5	.376	6.148	.000 **
	GRI G4 level	5.775	5	1.155	6.572	.000 **
Org type * Industry category	Reporting consistency	1.671	9	.186	3.037	.002 **
	GRI G4 level	3.042	9	.338	1.923	.047 *
Error	Reporting consistency	23.288	381	.061		
	GRI G4 level	66.964	381	.176		
Total	Reporting consistency	311.223	398			
	GRI G4 level	115.000	398			
Corrected total	Reporting consistency	29.024	397			
	GRI G4 level	81.771	397			

a. $R^2 = .198$ (Adjusted $R^2 = .164$)
b. $R^2 = .181$ (Adjusted $R^2 = .147$)

We followed up our statistical analysis with a structured review of sustainability reports from select organizations of different sizes and from different economic regions and industries. We selected only those reports which used the latest GRI G4 standards. The qualitative review did not provide sufficient information of whether these companies had adopted all the elements of the "ReSOLVE" framework to move towards adoption of CE concepts. Therefore, we are not able to conclude whether or not improved sustainability reporting and disclosures are leading towards adoption of CE concepts.

Discussion

Sustainability reporting makes abstract issues tangible and concrete, and assists in understanding and managing the effects of sustainability developments on the

Table 8.5 Tukey's post-hoc test on consistent reporting index and GRI G4 level for organization type

Dependent variable	(I) Org type	(J) Org type	Mean difference (I–J)	Std. error	Sig.
Consistent reporting index	Large	MNE	-.117989*	.0278049	.000
		SME	.196666*	.0477396	.000
	MNE	Large	.117989*	.0278049	.000
		SME	.314655*	.0506852	.000
	SME	Large	-.196666*	.0477396	.000
		MNE	-.314655*	.0506852	.000
GRI G4 level	Large	MNE	.20*	.047	.000
		SME	-.35*	.081	.000
	MNE	Large	-.20*	.047	.000
		SME	-.54*	.086	.000
	SME	Large	.35*	.081	.000
		MNE	.54*	.086	.000

Based on observed means.
The error term is: Mean square (error) = .176.
* The mean difference is significant at the .05 level.

organization's activities and strategy (GRI, 2013). Our premise has been that such voluntary initiatives are expected to provide insights to organizations' leaderships on how to adapt their business models and integrate their business models with that of others in the ecosystem, leading to realization of the CE principles.

While voluntary sustainability reporting frameworks like GRI have been criticized by some researchers for their inability to reveal the complete truth about sustainability of business practices within organizations (Fonseca et al., 2014), our detailed analysis of data over the period 2008–2017 on sustainability reports from different organizations – from multinationals to SMEs, and from all industry sectors – reveals that out of 10,126 organizations that publish sustainability reports, 398 are from India. We find that reporting practices are not concentrated in specific organization types or specific industries. However, the level of participation in India differs across organization types. While GRI sustainability reporting remains completely voluntary, an increasing number of Indian companies are joining the practice, suggesting GRI's acceptance as a meaningful framework and the leaderships' willingness to bring in a culture of sustainability thinking within the organization. In addition, reviewing the content of select reports from various Indian organizations, and the evolution of reporting frameworks over the years, we do not find strong evidence for the arguments posited by Fonseca et al. (2014) or Levy et al. (2010) – that GRI based reporting can mislead decision-makers as well as external stakeholders, and can camouflage unsustainable practices.

Table 8.6 Tukey's post-hoc test on reporting consistency for industry category

Dependent variable	(I) Industry category	(J) Industry category	Mean difference (I–J)	Std. error	Sig.
Consistent reporting index	Agriculture	Conglomerates	-.035696	.1138671	1.000
		Extractive industries	-.030135	.1097251	1.000
		Manufacturing	-.072960	.1030281	.981
		Others	-.162281	.1086089	.668
		Services	-.187884	.1028551	.450
	Conglomerates	Agriculture	.035696	.1138671	1.000
		Extractive industries	.005562	.0680486	1.000
		Manufacturing	-.037264	.0566199	.986
		Others	-.126584	.0662337	.397
		Services	-.152188	.0563045	.077
	Extractive industries	Agriculture	.030135	.1097251	1.000
		Conglomerates	-.005562	.0680486	1.000
		Manufacturing	-.042826	.0477461	.947
		Others	-.132146	.0588284	.219
		Services	-.157749*	.0473716	.012
	Manufacturing	Agriculture	.072960	.1030281	.981
		Conglomerates	.037264	.0566199	.986
		Extractive industries	.042826	.0477461	.947
		Others	-.089320	.0451217	.356
		Services	-.114924*	.0286228	.001
	Others	Agriculture	.162281	.1086089	.668
		Conglomerates	.126584	.0662337	.397
		Extractive industries	.132146	.0588284	.219
		Manufacturing	.089320	.0451217	.356
		Services	-.025603	.0447253	.993
	Services	Agriculture	.187884	.1028551	.450
		Conglomerates	.152188	.0563045	.077
		Extractive industries	.157749*	.0473716	.012
		Manufacturing	.114924*	.0286228	.001
		Others	.025603	.0447253	.993

Based on observed means.
The error term is: Mean square (error) = .176.
* The mean difference is significant at the .05 level.

Table 8.7 Tukey's post-hoc test on GRI G4 level for industry category

Dependent variable	(I) Industry category	(J) Industry category	Mean difference (I–J)	Std. error	Sig.
GRI G4 level	Agriculture	Conglomerates	.18	.193	.935
		Extractive industries	.11	.186	.993
		Manufacturing	.10	.175	.992
		Others	.34	.184	.430
		Services	.31	.174	.466
	Conglomerates	Agriculture	-.18	.193	.935
		Extractive industries	-.08	.115	.986
		Manufacturing	-.08	.096	.960
		Others	.16	.112	.710
		Services	.13	.095	.736
	Extractive industries	Agriculture	-.11	.186	.993
		Conglomerates	.08	.115	.986
		Manufacturing	.00	.081	1.000
		Others	.24	.100	.171
		Services	.21	.080	.102
	Manufacturing	Agriculture	-.10	.175	.992
		Conglomerates	.08	.096	.960
		Extractive industries	.00	.081	1.000
		Others	.24*	.077	.022
		Services	.21*	.049	.000
	Others	Agriculture	-.34	.184	.430
		Conglomerates	-.16	.112	.710
		Extractive industries	-.24	.100	.171
		Manufacturing	-.24*	.077	.022
		Services	-.03	.076	.999
	Services	Agriculture	-.31	.174	.466
		Conglomerates	-.13	.095	.736
		Extractive industries	-.21	.080	.102
		Manufacturing	-.21*	.049	.000
		Others	.03	.076	.999

Based on observed means.
The error term is: Mean square (error) = .176.
* The mean difference is significant at the .05 level.

Table 8.8 Longitudinal break-up of GRI reporting – globally and in India

Year	2008	2009	2010	2011	2012	2013	2014	2015	2016	2017
GRI G4	NA	NA	NA	NA	NA	56	1057	2348	3126	2254
Other	1314	1673	2266	3384	4017	4560	5077	5494	5982	5024
Total	1314	1673	2266	3384	4017	4616	6134	7842	9108	7278
GRI G4 %	NA	NA	NA	NA	NA	1%	17%	30%	34%	31%
GRI G4 – India	NA	NA	NA	NA	NA	1	21	52	80	48
Other – India	24	26	29	52	53	70	59	47	67	257
Total	24	26	29	52	53	71	80	99	147	305
GRI G4 India %	NA	NA	NA	NA	NA	1%	26%	53%	54%	16%

From our longitudinal study on organizations' disclosures, we notice significant improvement in disclosure practices over time. This has been possible due to improvement in the reporting framework itself – GRI has undergone several revisions over the past decade, making GRI G4, the latest GRI standards, much more specific and insightful for the stakeholders to review. In addition, our review of reports finds that the continuous reporting activities by organizations have led to improved processes and better thought processes among the executives and managers about how to achieve sustainability objectives.

The above observation brings us to our third research question – how close are we to CE. While CE has been talked about in various forums, and in certain industries and organizations it has been implemented to a reasonable extent, the true promise of CE remains unachievable unless the industry as a whole transforms itself around the way value is created. This is where we find a significant disconnect between sustainability reporting practices and achieving CE advantages. We observe that the circular economy is a larger construct where players across the business ecosystems need to coordinate and collaborate with aligned objectives. The concept of CE identifies waste in businesses as wasted resources, wasted lifecycle, wasted capacity, and wasted embedded value. The solution to reduce this waste lies in a circular supply chain, recovery and recycling, product life extension, sharing platforms and servicification of products – i.e. providing services that would otherwise be met by products (Lacy & Rutqvist, 2016). Significant transformation of existing business models is essential to ensuring sustainable consumption and production (Schroeder et al., 2019). Advancing the argument proposed by Vigneau et al. (2015) and Murray et al. (2017), we recommend further enhancements to the current GRI framework to provide for reporting on such collaboration in the areas of planning, resourcing, procurement, production, and reprocessing among organizations and customers in the business ecosystem. In addition, the framework should enable actionizing within the business ecosystem of the organization, so that decision-makers and collaboration partners can take corrective actions to realize CE promises.

Conclusion

This chapter contributes to developing insights about how leadership teams and boards in Indian organizations are undertaking sustainability reporting practices, and transitioning to adopting CE concepts. Sustainability reporting and disclosures help an organization identify the impact of its business footprint on social, environmental and economic spheres, and consequently the organization can develop plans to address these. By sharing information with all stakeholders, including regulators and the larger community, the leadership team ensures review and improvement of operational processes and governance, and introduces systems and mechanisms to capture necessary information that not only helps in reporting but also helps in progressive adaptation of the business model.

GRI-based sustainability disclosures have become the norm for many nations and industries, thanks to demands from shareholders and secondary stakeholders. Adoption of reporting practices and improvement in reporting quality do contribute to accountability and transparency. However, mere reporting lends to only peripheral changes in business models and many companies do not truly move towards sustainable business models, which requires drastic transformation. Consequently, we propose that in order to attain the promised benefits of CE, the leadership and the board may have to improve their deliberations on sustainability, or else reporting frameworks such as GRI should be enhanced to encourage companies and industries to work towards the transformation of business models for sustainable practices.

Note

1 www.globalreporting.org/information/about-gri/Pages/default.aspx

References and further reading

Aras, G., & Crowther, D. (2009). Making sustainable development sustainable. *Management Decision*, 47(6), 975–988.

Bocken, N., Short, S., Rana, P., & Evans, S. (2013). A value mapping tool for sustainable business modelling. *Corporate Governance*, 13(5), 482–497.

Brennan, N. M., & Merkl-Davies, D. M. (2014). Rhetoric and argument in social and environmental reporting: The Dirty Laundry case. *Accounting, Auditing & Accountability Journal*, 27(4), 602–633.

Cho, C. H., Laine, M., Roberts, R. W., & Rodrigue, M. (2015). Organized hypocrisy, organizational façades, and sustainability reporting. *Accounting, Organizations and Society*, 40(Jan), 78–94.

De Angelis, R. (2018). *Business Models in the Circular Economy: Concepts, Examples and Theory*. Cham, Switzerland: Palgrave Macmillan.

Demil, B., & Lecocq, X. (2010). Business model evolution: In search of dynamic consistency. *Long Range Planning*, 43(2–3), 227–246.

EMF (Ellen MacArthur Foundation) (2015). *Towards a Circular Economy: Business Rationale for an Accelerated Transition*. Available at: www.ellenmacarthurfoundation.org/publications/towards-a-circular-economy-business-rationale-for-an-accelerated-transition. Last accessed July 1 2018.

Fernandez-Feijoo, B., Romero, S., & Ruiz, S. (2014). Effect of stakeholders' pressure on transparency of sustainability reports within the GRI framework. *Journal of Business Ethics*, 122(1), 53–63.

Fonseca, A., McAllister, M. L., & Fitzpatrick, P. (2014). Sustainability reporting among mining corporations: A constructive critique of the GRI approach. *Journal of Cleaner Production*, 84(Dec), 70–83.

GRI (2013). *Sustainability Reporting Guidelines: G4*. Available at: www.globalreporting.org/resourcelibrary/GRIG4-Part1-Reporting-Principles-and-Standard-Disclosures.pdf. Last accessed 19 May 2019.

Hahn, R., & Lülfs, R. (2014). Legitimizing negative aspects in GRI-oriented sustainability reporting: A qualitative analysis of corporate disclosure strategies. *Journal of Business Ethics*, 123(3), 401–420.

Hall, J., & Wagner, M. (2012). Integrating sustainability into firms' processes: Performance effects and the moderating role of business models and innovation. *Business Strategy and the Environment*, 21(3), 183–196.

ITC (2018). *Sustainability Report 2018*. ITC Ltd. Available at www.itcportal.com/sustainability/sustainability-report-2018/sustainability-report-2018.pdf. Last accessed 7 April 2019.

Lacy, P., & Rutqvist, J. (2016). *Waste to Wealth: The Circular Economy Advantage*. New York: Palgrave Macmillan.

Levy, D. L., Brown, H. S., & De Jong, M. (2010). The contested politics of corporate governance: The case of the global reporting initiative. *Business & Society*, 49(1), 88–115.

Milne, M. J., & Gray, R. (2013). W(h)ither ecology? The triple bottom line, the global reporting initiative, and corporate sustainability reporting. *Journal of Business Ethics*, 118(1), 13–29.

Murray, A., Skene, K., & Haynes, K. (2017). The circular economy: An interdisciplinary exploration of the concept and application in a global context. *Journal of Business Ethics*, 140(3), 369–380.

Schroeder, P., Anggraeni, K., & Weber, U. (2019). The relevance of circular economy practices to the sustainable development goals. *Journal of Industrial Ecology*, 23(1), 77–95.

Vigneau, L., Humphreys, M., & Moon, J. (2015). How do firms comply with international sustainability standards? Processes and consequences of adopting the global reporting initiative. *Journal of Business Ethics*, 131(2), 469–486.

Part III

Summary

Learning from the Indian experience

9 Learning from the Indian experience

Towards better governance

Summarizing the role of boards in Indian corporate governance

In Chapter 2 we discussed the four key elements of corporate governance: transparency, responsibility, accountability, and fairness. The board has to ensure timely, adequate, and accurate disclosure of all material information to interested and impacted parties. The board also has to take responsibility for its decisions. These decisions need to be balanced, taking into consideration its obligations and accountability to the shareholders and other stakeholders. In addition, the board needs to demonstrate fairness and equitable treatment to all shareholders.

Given that boards are the primary players in ensuring better corporate governance, our analyses in Part II of this book centred on three key aspects: board composition, contribution and compensation, and how they contribute to value creation for the firms.

The analysis of board and performance data from 200 listed Indian companies that form the NSE's Nifty200 index covering a 20-year period provides interesting insights. We find that diversity of the board, measured through the presence of female directors, and limiting the influence of promoter directors do contribute to positive performance for the companies. It is often argued that the presence of female board members brings balance to the board composition, promotes diversity in the thought processes of the board, and conveys a sense of good corporate governance and a firm's ethical behaviour. We find support for this argument in our empirical analysis. One of the recommendations of the Uday Kotak Committee to SEBI in 2017 suggested that it was not sufficient that the board had a female director; the board must also have at least one female independent director. This would probably further enhance diversity of thoughts and ideas in board deliberations.

The Indian regulators and various committees constituted to date to improve corporate governance in the country have been stressing the importance of the presence of independent directors on the board, who have no pecuniary relationship with the company or the owners. It is expected that professionally qualified independent directors are able to bring in fairness in decision-making, improve quality of decisions, and take into consideration the expectations of shareholders, including minority shareholders, and other stake-holders. However, we find that the higher presence of independent directors does not benefit firms as far as value creation is concerned. This brings us to a critical question: are Indian boards still "ceremonial boards"? A ceremonial board, as suggested by Charan (2011), is driven by the CEO's agenda, with no productive dialogue in the boardroom, where the management tightly controls information flow, and the independent directors tend to approve all of the CEO's proposals. We surmise that the independent directors may need to liberate themselves from the clutches of an all-powerful CEO / MD, make sense of information pertaining to decision-making, focus on material issues, and contribute to value-creation for the firm through involvement and superior decision-making. Such a transition would make Indian boards, as Charan (2011) puts it, "progressive".

Additionally, the Uday Kotak Committee also suggested to SEBI in 2017 that there should not be any board-interlocks, i.e. an executive director and an independent director of a company cannot play reverse roles in the board of another company. Such provisions would ensure that independent directors on the board are truly independent.

When it comes to the contribution and involvement of board members, we observe that directors' participation in board meetings has a positive effect on several firm performance parameters. However, the average participation in board meetings in Indian companies is abysmally low. From the data it appears that board members, executive or independent, consider their board positions more as titular than as a responsibility. Section 167 (1) (b) of CA2013 provides that if a director absents himself from all the meetings of the board for a period of 12 months or more, with or without the leave of the board, she / he shall be deemed to have vacated her / his office. This provision in CA2013 may not be sufficient to have an engaged board – the board members may decide to attend just one meeting in a year, and their contribution would be virtually nil, considering prolonged absence and lack of involvement.

A related data point, directors' presence in other companies' boards, brings deeper insights into why board members are lacking in participation in board meetings. If a director is present on other companies' boards, they should have a broader perspective of business challenges and opportunities, and be able to cross-pollinate ideas. However, excessive participation, i.e. a director is present on a large number of boards, can be detrimental too. We observe that the average number of boards where a director is also a director elsewhere is extremely high in Indian companies. Further investigation suggests that a large number of directors, especially independent directors, have agreed to participate in a large number of company boards, across geography and industry sectors. This can be truly taxing on them, and they may not be able to do justice to their roles in most of the companies. The Uday Kotak Committee's recommendations to SEBI could definitely help to alleviate this situation. The committee recommended that by April 2020 the maximum number of boards where a director of a listed company can participate should be seven.

Board-level committees are important forums of the board where deep deliberations, debates, and analysis are supposed to take place. CA2013 mandates at least four board-level committees: an audit committee, nomination and remuneration committee, stakeholders' relationship committee, and a risk management committee for large companies. In terms of participation in board-level committees, our empirical data and analysis results provide two insights: (a) the number of directors who are members of any committee is very low, suggesting that many directors, on average, do not participate in any committees; and (b) directors' presence in committees has no influence on firm performance. As the average participation in board-level committees by directors is very low, we cannot draw any meaningful conclusions on this factor.

We also find that CEO duality, i.e. the CEO / MD performing the role of chairperson of the board, has negative impact on several performance measures, suggesting the presence of agency effect and weakening of the power of the other directors in such situations. While CA2013 recommends that there should be strict segregation of roles of the CEO / MD and the chairperson, the Uday Kotak Committee has a more stringent recommendation: it would not be sufficient that the chairperson is a non-executive director, the chairperson must not be related to the MD / CEO as per the definition of "relative" in CA2013. This would again ensure that proxy CEO duality is abolished and prevent concentration of executive power.

In terms of directors' compensation, we find that total remuneration to the directors has a positive influence on firm performance measures. This suggests that superior remuneration may lead to a higher sense of responsibility and sense of ownership in the directors, and these, in turn, may lead to superior, value-creating decisions in the board.

When we conduct our empirical analysis specifically on the SOEs, using the same models, we find similar results. Higher presence of independent directors, directors' presence in board meetings, directors' presence in other companies' boards, directors' remuneration, and directors' participation in board-level committees positively influence one or more performance measures. This clearly suggests that SOEs, despite their social roles and meeting the mandates of the government, are in a position to create superior value as business entities with superior corporate governance parameters.

Summarizing the role of shareholders, regulators and other stakeholders

Role and rights of shareholders

Shareholders, being the owners of the company, engage the board as their custodians, to protect their wealth, and help create value. As evident from our discussion in Chapter 3 and findings in Chapter 6, both the MCA and SEBI have instituted several effective measures to protect shareholders' interests. For example, CA2013 and its subsequent amendments provide for shareholders' approval on several statutory matters, including related party transactions, investments and borrowings beyond specified thresholds, executive remuneration beyond prescribed thresholds, sale of an undertaking of the company, amendment of the constitutional documents of the company, and issue of new shares. In addition, under CA2013, small shareholders can seek the appointment of a minority shareholder representative on the board of a listed company, and a director can even be removed by shareholders through an ordinary resolution. If board performance evaluation is made available to shareholders, as per CA2013, then it may not be difficult for the shareholders to identify an ineffective director and seek his / her removal. The act also allows shareholders to initiate class action lawsuits against the company and its directors. A group of shareholders who collectively own more than 10 per cent of voting rights can demand a general meeting of shareholders as well.

Apart from CA2013, SEBI's LODR clauses also provide for protection of investors' interests. Some of the key requirements stipulated by SEBI are in the areas of disclosure, which helps address the information asymmetry between the company, the board, and the shareholders. Some of the recent enhancements that have come in through the Uday Kotak Committee include disclosure of board members' skills and expertise, mandatory disclosure on related party transactions, observations on board evaluation, including action taken on board evaluation, mandatory publication of quarterly financial numbers, and disclosure of medium-term and long-term strategy in the management discussion section of the annual report.

SEBI's SCORES application is another mechanism through which individual investors can seek redress. Going by the volume of queries and statuses of resolution, it appears that SCORES is an effective and useful application for investors.

Thus, we may conclude that in the past two decades the shareholders of publicly listed companies have been given due importance, so they may get to know about their company's operations and governance, and provisions have been created for them to take on an erring board. However, as we have seen in Chapter 7, in the case of Coal India, the institutional investor, despite reasonable arguments, could not bring about any change in the way the company was governed.

Role of regulators

The MCA is the primary statutory body responsible for framing company laws in the country, and the introduction of CA2013, which is a major overhaul of the old Companies Act 1956, has been one of the defining movements by the ministry to address the growing concerns over the poor quality of corporate governance. In particular, in the wake of Satyam Computer Services scandal that rocked the reputation of the Indian business landscape, it was necessary to frame strict regulations to address the prevailing governance issues across Indian companies.

SEBI, the statutory regulatory authority for companies listed in stock markets, operates alongside the MCA's regulations, to bring in additional conditions to publicly traded companies in India. In the past 20 years SEBI had instituted several committees to transform corporate governance practices in these companies. SEBI's LODR has been amended several times, based on the inputs of these committees.

An interesting concern came up during the implementation of the Uday Kotak Committee's recommendations to SEBI. The MCA, being the ministry in charge of company laws, found that SEBI was probably overstepping its statutory role by bringing in clauses in the LODR that were harsher and stricter than those already present in CA2013. For example, the committee recommended that there must be at least one female independent director in the board. The MCA's contention was that this might be too strict and CA2013 already insists on a female director, executive or non-executive. In fact the MCA, in its observation, went on to say that such strict clauses in SEBI's LODR might not benefit India's attempt to improve its position in the "Ease of doing business" index ranking. It is expected that the MCA and SEBI will collaborate more in the coming months.

Role and rights of other stakeholders

In Chapter 8 we studied how Indian companies are approaching becoming sustainable businesses. By bringing in the concepts of sustainability, companies and their boards recognize the importance and needs of other stakeholders who are impacted by the company's business.

As companies realize that sustainable business practices are essential for their own value creation, it is expected that other stakeholders' voices will be heard by the boards more often and that board members will adopt practices that do not jeopardize the interests of other stakeholders.

Concluding remarks

We may still have some sceptics today who would question the role of superior corporate governance practices. Past research, as well our own empirical studies covered in this book, provides robust evidence that firms with sound governance parameters exhibit significantly greater returns when compared to companies with weaker governance parameters. In fact, well-governed companies across the world command a premium in the market. Our research highlights the importance of: (a) composition of boards, especially their independence in law and in spirit from the company's management; (b) contribution and involvement of the board; (c) compensation of the board. We have also studied the role of corporate governance parameters in the performance of SOEs, and if and how corporate governance has changed since the introduction of CA2013. In addition, our empirical studies involve limited analysis of data pertaining to protecting shareholder interests, and how the boards and leadership are moving towards sustainable business models to address the interests of the larger stakeholder community.

While we find that regulations have significantly improved over time, resulting in better composition of the board, and improved disclosures, leading to reduced risks for the business as well as investors, we still do not see evidence of progressive boards where the directors work closely as a team, leverage information and focus their attention on substantive issues.

One of the aspects of Indian corporate governance that has not been analysed in this book is how Indian boards are being evaluated and how their performance evolves both individually and as a team. We invite readers to review a study conducted by InGovern (2016) on top the 100 companies in India on this subject. We also would have liked to deep-dive into the activities of board committees; however, this could not be done due to the lack of large-scale historical data.

To conclude, with rigorous legal and statutory frameworks, corporate governance practices in India are bound to improve, and we are already seeing some early results. We are certain the country will demonstrate leading practices in several areas of corporate governance in the coming years.

References and further reading

Charan, R. (2011). *Boards that Deliver: Advancing Corporate Governance from Compliance to Competitive Advantage (Vol. 20)*. Hoboken, NJ: John Wiley & Sons.

InGovern (2016). *Report on Board Evaluation Practices by Top 100 Companies.* InGovern. Available at: www.ingovern.com/2016/05/report-on-board-evaluation-practices-by-top-100-companies/. Last accessed 7 April 2019.

Index

Note: Page numbers in *italics* refer to figures; page numbers in **bold** refer to tables.

Printed in the United States
by Baker & Taylor Publisher Services